D1443783

RUNNING

with My HEAD

DOWN

RUNNING
with My HEAD
DOWN

AN ENTREPRENEUR'S STORY *of* PASSION, PERSEVERANCE, *and* PURPOSE

Frank V. Fiume II

GREENLEAF
BOOK GROUP PRESS

Published by Greenleaf Book Group Press
Austin, Texas
www.gbgpress.com

Distributed by Greenleaf Book Group

For ordering information or special discounts for bulk purchases, please contact Greenleaf Book Group at PO Box 91869, Austin, TX 78709, 512.891.6100.

Design and composition by Greenleaf Book Group and Sheila Parr
Cover design by Greenleaf Book Group and Sheila Parr

Publisher's Cataloging-in-Publication data is available.

Print ISBN: 978-1-62634-641-3

eBook ISBN: 978-1-62634-642-0

Part of the Tree Neutral® program, which offsets the number of trees consumed in the production and printing of this book by taking proactive steps, such as planting trees in direct proportion to the number of trees used: www.treeneutral.com

TreeNeutral

Printed in the United States of America on acid-free paper

19 20 21 22 23 24   10 9 8 7 6 5 4 3 2 1

First Edition

To Nadine and our incredible children, Taylor-Marie and Frankie—and to future generations of our family who aspire to make their imprint on the world.

CONTENTS

THE QUEST FOR PURPOSE

What am I meant to do with my life?

What is my destiny?

How am I going to get there?

These were some of the age-old questions that most preoccupied me from adolescence through young adulthood.

When I was in doubt about my future, I'd repeatedly turn to my dad for his advice. As I think back on it now, I was really asking him: What is my *purpose* in life?

Dad, who was a self-confident, successful medical professional at a prestigious Manhattan hospital, would always respond to my question in the same reassuring way: "Don't worry about it. You'll figure it out."

But how?

I had this insane misconception that I would wake up one day and have a life-altering epiphany. I figured I'd hear the voice of God telling me exactly what to do with my life—like something out of the movies. But it never happened. When I was a naïve college student, it seemed to me as if the happiest people were the ones who had found this "Holy Grail of Purpose." I envied the students who knew what they wanted to major in and what they wanted to be. I assumed that those of us who hadn't figured this out were doomed to struggle emotionally and financially.

I put a lot of pressure on myself, wanting to find out *why* I was put on this earth. How would I know when I found that purpose? What if it was too difficult to attain? Who would help me get there? I believed that once I found my purpose, it would lead me from poverty to success.

> # "THERE IS NO MAGIC ANSWER OR FORMULA."

But what I learned is that there is no magic answer or formula. The trajectory of success is a zigzag, not a straight line. And that's why finding your purpose in life is never the result of just one event or decision. You'll find that lessons accumulate as experience grows, and your mission changes as priorities shift. You may strike out on one pathway, but you will often correct your course as you go. You'll find that the joyful—and sometimes painful—events of life ultimately change your route, sharpen your focus, and move you in unexpected directions.

In my case, I eventually *did* figure out what I was meant to do, though it took decades of trial and error.

I was strongly influenced by my father, who chose to ride the ups and downs at the same hospital for thirty years with his eye toward pension eligibility and retirement. While this model worked for him, it didn't match my entrepreneurial spirit. Of course, we're hugely influenced by our parents, so at first I conformed to Dad's vision *for* me; I went into medical equipment sales—even though I really wanted to work in sports management.

I made good money and achieved what I needed to achieve, but I found myself locked in golden handcuffs, doing a job I hated. After years of frustration, I finally broke free to follow my true passion, which was to build a sports company and prove to myself that I could get to where I was meant to be. In the pages that follow, you'll learn exactly how I did it, who inspired me, and how I identified a passion that led to a multimillion-dollar business. Most important, you'll see what lessons I learned along the way and how they can be applied to any business or life experience.

In the end, finding your purpose is about making your own breaks and creating your own luck. Part of the fun of creating any business is not merely reaching the destination—it's the journey itself. It was the climb *up* the mountain—not just reaching the summit—that was so exciting to me.

And even after I created what became a national organization with hundreds of franchisees and employees, I found out that business is much more than merely achieving performance goals or acquiring things.

It's about believing wholeheartedly in your cause, evolving from one mission to another as you mature, and achieving your life's purpose—while helping others to achieve theirs, since true fulfillment comes not from solely profiting for yourself, but by contributing to the success of others.

•   •   •

In the pages that follow, I share my personal story, not to demonstrate how to discover your life's purpose, but to show you how *it* will find you. That purpose will keep whispering in your ear. And you have to listen to that voice, being always conscious and aware of what your heart and intuitions are trying to tell you. Believe me, you have a gift, and it's that voice that will lead you to it. Ready or not, it's up to you to accept the challenge of discovering your destiny—with an unstoppable hunger.

You will be able to do that by ignoring the doubters and naysayers (including yourself), by consistently summoning up the determination to face the obstacles life will inevitably throw at you, and by determining what you want to do to achieve the true secret to happiness in life: fulfillment.

A FINAL NOTE ABOUT THE TRUTH

As I set out to capture my business experience in words, I was faced with the decision about how candid I wanted to be. When telling a story, we all have at least two versions. The first is the sugarcoated account we tell most people, skimming over the rough parts and presenting a sweetened, sanitized history of what happened. And then there's the real version of the story: a straightforward look at how the events of life have impacted us. That's the one I'm going to tell you: the truth uncovered one layer at a time.

Frank V. Fiume II
October 2019

IN THE QUEST FOR PURPOSE

- Lessons accumulate as experience grows.
- Your mission changes as priorities shift.
- You may strike out on one pathway, but you will often correct your course as you go.
- The joyful—and sometimes painful—events of life ultimately change your route, sharpen your focus, and move you in unexpected directions.
- You make your own breaks and create your own luck.
- Your purpose will keep whispering in your ear. Listen to that voice and be aware of what your heart and intuitions are trying to tell you.

ACKNOWLEDGMENTS

First and foremost, I want to thank the love of my life, my wife, Nadine, for her love and support through all the years of our lives, and our two cubs, Taylor-Marie and Frankie, who are the center of our world.

To my mom: Your love, encouragement, and belief in me since my earliest childhood memory is the very foundation of what gave me the strength to persevere through all the chapters of my life.

To my dad, my first hero, who supported and guided me as I looked up to you in the search for purpose: We sometimes marched to the beat of different drums, but the one constant was our love for one another.

To my sister, Donna: Your love and belief in me from the time we were little have always given me strength, and you have been a source of love I could always count on.

To my brother-in-law, Rob: You were my first unofficial business coach back in the day and someone who talked me off the ledge more times than I can remember.

To my niece, Madison, and nephews, Aaron (A. J.) and Bobby: My hope is that you will read something in the following pages that will give you the inner strength to fulfill your life purpose—with focus, determination, and passion.

To my uncle, Larry Puleo—one of the few people who believed

in my vision for a softball league and stood behind it right from the start: Your utter confidence in me gave me added strength to pursue my dream. The family and parenting philosophy that you and Aunt Marilyn demonstrated has been an inspiration to Nadine and me.

I'm deeply thankful to Brian Sanders, my mentor, business colleague, and friend, and one of the most inspirational and astute business executives I've ever known. His unwavering vision and commitment as company president (and later CEO) gave me something I can never repay: extra time to spend with my family.

How can I thank someone who has been the heart and soul of i9 Sports and my first and most-trusted employee: Kim Armellino! Your dedication, honesty, and intuition are the biggest reasons our company survived and thrived.

As far as the production of this book is concerned, a huge thanks to best-selling author Glenn Plaskin. Your literary skill, insight, and help in writing the story of my journey made it an unbelievable experience, and one that was unexpectedly therapeutic.

To my franchise mentors, Joe Mathews, of the Franchise Performance Group, who saved our company when it was going down in a blaze of glory, and Mark Siebert, of the iFranchise Group, who was with me from our humble beginnings to the time I sold the company. Without both of you, this story would have had a drastically different ending.

To current and former i9 Sports and ABA Sports employees: Alli Wentzell, April Thomas, Brandy Zickefoose, Cary Linkfield, Charla Alma, Chris Dietrich, Elissa Lindsey, Erica Duncan, Geoff Gilliece, Jennifer Gordon, Jennifer Rodriguez, Jennifer Spinella, Justin Phillips, Kelvyn Hemphill, Kevin Brandt, Mike Carty, Owen Waldrep, Scott Matson, Scott Morgenroth, Susan Rabel, Tom Filgate, and the late Chip Parsons: Without you, and most of all our franchisees, my vision for i9 would never have come to fruition.

To my attorneys, Stan Bulua and Joe Dunn, my CPA, Bill Boyette, and my advisors, Alex Meshechok, Alex Mumblat, Richard Harmon,

Ajay Gupta, Darsi McCarthy, Brian Jenkins, and Alex Mazza: I am forever grateful for all of your guidance and help in completing my mission at i9 Sports. And Richard, I am indebted to you for introducing me to Tony Robbins.

To my personal life coach, Sara Basloe, who has expertly guided and supported me, helping me to "move mountains" and holding me accountable for all the goals I set for myself.

And finally, a heartfelt thank-you to the one and only Tony Robbins, who has inspired me to live a life of fulfillment far beyond what I could have imagined. Thanks to the many seminars of his that I've attended, I know that my destiny was shaped by my *decisions*, and not my conditions. There's no question that without Tony's wisdom, much of what I describe in this book never would have been possible.

PART ONE

Chapter One

RUNNING WITH
MY HEAD DOWN

Babe Ruth always said that every strike brought him closer to the next home run. And I think the same about the success of an entrepreneur. Yes, there are times when you'll swing and miss and even get knocked down. But if you can get up again and face the next pitch, you'll learn a lesson you never would have.

In baseball, one of the first things you learn is that, after hitting the ball, you put your head down and run from home plate to first base as fast as you can without letting anything distract you. I use that baseball image as a metaphor for my life and the life of a business.

All businesses ride the rapids. Up and down they go, pulled inevitably by the currents of fate and circumstance. Every company has financial highs and lows, company secrets that nobody knows, disappointments, resentments, ugly moments—and, of course, moments of victory and triumph. No business is a smooth ride. No matter how perfect things might look on the outside, it's never a true picture of reality. My company was no exception.

LIVING IN A COMFORT ZONE WAS NOT MY GOAL

When I started my first business, a local Long Island adult men's softball league, I knew nobody; I was given no breaks; I had no money. Plenty of people gave me every reason why I wouldn't be successful.

Back then, I was competing against established league owners who had a market monopoly and wanted to squash a young upstart like me. So, when I went to them for advice about starting a league of my own, they told me to forget it, that it was hopeless for a newcomer like me to break into the industry. They were the pros; I was an amateur. I would never find playing fields or new customers—they seemed to have a stranglehold on all of it. My dad was skeptical and told me to stick to selling medical equipment or I'd screw up my life. He also did not approve of me pursuing a professional sports management career or a law degree. All this negativity reinforced the notion that I should just stick to the safe and familiar—and that if I didn't, I'd fail.

> "I WANTED TO TAKE RISKS, BREAK WITH CONVENTION, AND CREATE SOMETHING UNIQUE OF MY OWN."

Yet the idea of settling for a conventional job and staying stuck in it for the sake of security was not something I was willing to settle for. Living in a comfort zone was not my goal. In fact, it was the antithesis of what I wanted my life to be—I wanted to take risks, break with convention, and create something unique of my own.

THE MAKING OF A REBEL

What was driving my appetite for success? As you'll see, my parents eventually split up, and there would be years of financial deprivation when my mom, my sister, and I moved like gypsies from one rental apartment to another. As the bills piled up and my mom worked two jobs just to keep us going, I vowed that this would never happen to my family again. So yes, there was fire in my belly. My passion had also been stoked by the teachers, coaches, and other adults who had underestimated me as a kid. And finally, my drive to succeed was fueled by the desire to prove myself to my dad. Like many other entrepreneurs, whatever drove my hunger at any given time, it made me a determined rebel.

"I WASN'T AFRAID TO FAIL."

No matter what my deficiencies, I compensated for them by expecting more from myself than anyone else could possibly expect from me. The high standard I set for myself became my greatest asset. I wasn't afraid to fail—because I was so hungry to succeed.

The entrepreneurial spirit is about single-mindedly pursuing a vision and allowing nothing to detour it. That's the way I've approached every business I've ever been in: running with my head down, and taking one step at a time toward my goal.

SHEA STADIUM: WHERE IT ALL BEGAN

Some childhood memories stay with you forever. No matter how many years go by, you still think back to that one moment in time when you felt incredible happiness. For me, it was in the summer of 1973. I was four years old, and my parents took me to Shea Stadium for my first baseball game. On a beautiful, warm, sunny day, we walked the short distance from our nearby apartment through Flushing Meadow Park. I was in awe.

There we were, entering a mammoth, five-tiered stadium that seated nearly 60,000 fans. Flags whipped in the wind atop the stadium, signifying that the Mets had a home game. The building had a checkerboard design painted in Mets' orange and blue—the same colors as the seats and railings. With thousands of fans pouring in, the anticipation and energy of the crowd was electric. For a little kid, it was a magical sensory experience, complete with the smell of popcorn and hotdogs and the sight of vendors everywhere, hawking food, T-shirts, and baseball hats. Could there be a more perfect place? Not to me. It was love at first sight.

As we walked in, I was blown away by the perfection of the manicured field, the giant electronic scoreboard, the billboards in the outfield, and the rows and rows of seats. We made our way to the upper deck on the first-base side. Even now, I can replay in my mind almost every detail of that day. We were so high up that when the players ran onto the field, they looked like little ants. I sat on Dad's lap in anticipation of the action, and then it began. The announcer took to the microphone with his booming voice, and the crowd went wild.

From that day forward, much of my life would revolve around the game of baseball—watching it on TV, going to games, and playing it myself. In fact, my love of the game would affect everything I later did in my life—managing amateur leagues, creating a nationally franchised sports business, and running a corporation.

BASEBALL AND LIFE

After that first Mets game, Mom began buying me baseball cards, which became my obsession—especially after my parents' marriage began to deteriorate, around the time we moved from Corona, Queens, to a new house in Nesconset, Long Island. The house was located in a brand-new middle-class neighborhood. Shortly after we landed there, Dad became a fading presence—he spent most of his time at the Manhattan hospital where he worked as a cardiac technician.

That left me, age eight, my little sister Donna, and my mom largely alone—and with my mom extremely vulnerable financially. Looking back, I can now see that my growing fixation on sports was an escape from what was going on at home. In my child's mind, the initial absence of Dad made me feel a deep sense of disappointment, and for the first time, my confidence and sense of security was rattled. A year later, when my parents officially announced their divorce, I was both furious and sad at the same time.

As the first kid in my class to have divorced parents, I instantly became an outcast at school and with my neighborhood friends who perceived me as different. It left me feeling inadequate and unmotivated at school, and I struggled with poor grades. In fact, every year I was barely able to avoid getting left behind. If it hadn't been for summer school, I would have been held back for sure. Those were the terrible school years, as I put it—a devastating memory. I didn't feel my teachers (or my baseball coaches) believed in me. There was nothing about me that was particularly extraordinary, or at least nobody seemed to see it if there was. Everything led back to my parents separating.

But my drive to overachieve stemmed directly from this childhood pain, and without it, everything in my life might have been different: I might not have had the inner drive to prove myself and find my entrepreneurial purpose. In any case, by the time I was ten, I had become more introverted, a kid who was always distracted by things happening at home. Without Dad around, my world felt turned upside down. I'd had a secure and happy early childhood, but I now felt down on my luck. It was as if not just my family life was broken, but I was broken too. Everyone seemed better than me. What saved me from all this domestic drama? As always, it was baseball.

FIELD OF DREAMS: CREATING MY FIRST LEAGUE

During the summer of 1978, the Yankees were my escape in life. In the second half of the season, they came roaring back to force a one-game playoff against the Boston Red Sox. Bucky Dent's famous home run in the seventh inning put the Yankees ahead of the Red Sox to go to the playoffs—which led to another World Series confrontation versus the Los Angeles Dodgers. Moments like these were golden.

I wanted to stay up late to watch the World Series games, even though they were played on school nights. Mom wouldn't let me, but each morning I would wake up to see the score, scribbled on a piece of paper, by my bed. (My childhood hero, Graig Nettles, became the star of that series by making acrobatic catch after catch at third base, saving the Yankees and leading them to victory. It was an unforgettable World Series championship that cemented my lifelong love for the New York Yankees.)

Around this time, I started playing a board game that became my new escape from reality—All-Star Baseball.[1] This was essentially a simulation of major league games built around a spinner and player discs (a mix of then current players and all-time greats such as Babe Ruth). I'd play it day and night, creating teams and keeping track of all the statistics. My brain was always churning over the batting lineup, deciding whether the team should steal a base or not, and predicting the outcome of archrival matchups. I loved keeping the statistics and analyzing the probabilities. I would play a full 162-game season with playoffs and a World Series.

All the while, I'd also be watching Yankee games on TV and listening to the play-by-play radio broadcasting team of Phil Rizzuto, Frank Messer, and Bill White. I'd even talk like them as I announced the play-by-play results of my game. It wasn't only the scores and wins that fascinated me, but also the storylines about the teams and players. It was total immersion, and I felt as though I had found my calling.

Without realizing it, I was mastering the craft of creating a league. In fact, years later, I realized that I was following the so-called 10,000 Hour Rule—a principle that states that 10,000 hours of "deliberate practice" are needed for someone to become world-class in *any* field.

---

1   The game was manufactured by Cadaco-Ellis and designed by baseball player Ethan Allen. It first appeared in 1941, and a special version is still sold today.

It's a key trait among entrepreneurs—laser-focusing on your passion and chasing it with your head down.

My love of the game kicked up another notch when I realized the potential of our spacious, fenced-in backyard. When I was about nine, my baseball-supportive mom gave the OK for my friends and me to tear up our large backyard and turn it into a real baseball field, where we could play Wiffle ball, using a plastic bat and ball. We set to work building a pitcher's mound, an infield, the baselines, and even a warning track in the outfield. We built a dugout using two-by-fours and nails that we stole from nearby construction sites and then used chicken wire to make bat and ball holders. The field looked like something out of *The Sandlot*, a 1993 American coming-of-age baseball movie.

My backyard became the coolest place to hang out in the neighborhood. I kept statistics for all the kids in the neighborhood, tracking our home runs, strikeouts, and season scores. I was like the Shenandoah Boulevard league commissioner and team owner all in one. And that's how a fourth-grader began his managerial career in sports!

MAGIC IN THE UPPER DECKS

Needless to say, one of the absolute highlights of my childhood was when Mom took me to my first New York Yankees game for my eleventh birthday in September 1979. By that time, she was on her own without my father, so she didn't have much money and we had to sit way up in the upper decks on the first-base side.

But on that beautiful, clear day, there was something magical in the air, and I felt the same excitement I'd experienced at the first game I attended with my parents many years earlier. Just the smell and feel of the stadium was electric to me. None other than my hero Graig Nettles hit a walk-off, extra-inning home run in the bottom of the tenth to beat the rival Kansas City Royals! It couldn't have been any sweeter—the best birthday present imaginable.

Unfortunately, the previous month had proved to be a tragic one for the Yankees as they mourned the death of their captain, Thurman Munson, who was killed at age thirty-two in a plane crash. My friends and I worshipped him, and we were crushed. I'll never forget one of the boys sobbing as though he'd lost a family member. Munson was his hero.

Munson's death also had a profound effect on me because baseball was no longer just a game. It had become an all-consuming passion. My mom knew the game meant much more to me than just balls and strikes. Once I learned its history and traditions and understood who the players really were behind the uniform, baseball became ingrained in my soul. I spent the spring and fall playing Wiffle ball day and night with the neighborhood kids; summers playing Little League Baseball; and winters playing either tackle football—with no equipment, of course—or street hockey.

The next summer I went to a baseball camp, and my mind was blown away when Jim Spencer, first-baseman for the New York Yankees, showed up in uniform! I was in awe of the pinstripes, the reality of a professional player up close; he represented everything I aspired to, the highest standard and work ethic.

After that, if I wasn't studying baseball player statistics on the back of the 700-card set, I was watching the game on TV, playing it myself, or listening to it on the radio, where Phil Rizzuto made the game come to life with his colorful commentary. When the Yankees capitalized on the other team's mistake, Rizzuto would always say, "You make your own breaks." Years later, I realized what he said was true: Great things *do* happen when you take advantage of the moment, and good fortune isn't just luck; it's knowing how to capitalize on the opportunity at hand.

WINNING IS MORE THAN WINS AND LOSSES

There came a pivotal moment in my childhood when I realized you could take baseball *too* seriously—at least some of the parents could.

I was stunned to witness one overly competitive dad in our neighborhood who verbally abused his eleven-year-old son for walking in the winning run at his Little League championship game. This guy was over-the-top—yelling at his son and making him pitch for hours on end to the point of exhaustion as punishment for "losing the game." He was brutal, and he stripped away his son's enjoyment of baseball by turning it into a punishment.

This taught me a huge lesson—*parents* can get in the way and ruin the joy of the game by over-pressuring their kids. Why do they do it? Some of them were living their failed dreams through their children and had been deluded into thinking their kid was going to play ball professionally. The chance of that was 0.1 percent!

These parents failed to realize that baseball is more than just wins and losses. It's really about having fun and learning how to play the game; winning with grace and losing with dignity. To me, that's the key lesson in playing sports, one that I learned at age ten and would apply years later when I ran my own nationwide youth sports league.

WHEN YOU RUN WITH YOUR HEAD DOWN:

- You expect more from yourself than anyone else could possibly expect from you.
- You're so hungry to succeed, you're not afraid to fail.
- You aspire to the highest standards and work ethic.
- You make your own breaks.
- Great things happen when you take advantage of the moment.
- Good fortune isn't just luck; it's knowing how to capitalize on the opportunity at hand.
- Be ready to take risks, break with convention, and create something unique of your own.

Chapter Two

FALLING DOWN AND GETTING BACK UP

At age twelve, two years after my parents' divorce, reality set in: My mom's slumping finances left us no choice but to move out of our big house in Nesconset. On the last evening before we moved, I remember crying as I walked around my backyard Wiffle ball field, pulling out those two-by-four wooden bases and stuffing them, along with the yellow plastic bats and Wiffle balls, into black garbage bags. I knew full well that there would be no place to put them without a field of my own. It was devastating and a wrenching, painful change that represented another loss in my life.

Our next stop would be a tiny one-bedroom basement apartment in a single-family home in Whitestone, Queens—a definite downgrade in our lifestyle. It was a dark, creepy little place with a noisy landlord living above us. His racket radiated down on us through the cheap Styrofoam drop ceiling, which was anything but soundproof. I felt like my world was falling apart.

Yet, as kids often do, I adjusted quickly. When I arrived on the first day at my new junior high school, it was like landing on a different planet, with a rainbow of ethnicities. I soon made new friends, thanks to sports, which are always a common denominator. I also found a new obsession—a sports board game called Strat-O-Matic, a more advanced version of All-Star Baseball. It became my constant companion and an escape from what would become a very difficult life in Queens.

Over the course of fourteen years, we lived in seven apartments, at one point winding up in a borderline slum—a two-bedroom apartment on the first floor of a decrepit four-story brick building in College Point, Queens. A harsh blue fluorescent hallway light buzzed loudly and shone into our apartment day and night through our flimsy front door, which was made out of thin glass and cheap wood veneer. Anyone could have pushed it in at any moment. The toxic stench of bug spray wafted through the building, continuously and ineffectively battling an infestation of roaches that was like something out of a horror movie. Every time we turned on the kitchen light, dozens of roaches scampered up and down the walls and in and out of the cupboards. It was disgusting, and of all the places I lived in as a kid, that place was the one that most embarrassed me—and made me feel the most vulnerable.

Dad, on the other hand, was in another stratosphere.

He and his new wife were living in a lavish two-story, ranch-style house in Oceanside, Long Island, with an in-ground pool and a sprawling deck overlooking a canal—complete with a dock and a new twenty-five-foot boat. They had the best of everything. We, on the other hand, were living a very different kind of life. During the day, my mother worked as a clerk for the Catholic Youth Organization. At night, she developed film at Caleb Labs in Long Island City, and at one point, assembled switches in a lamp factory. We depended on the alimony and child support from my father, but even working two jobs, Mom struggled to make ends meet.

Every other weekend, Dad would pick my sister and me up in his brand-new, sporty silver Toyota Celica. We traveled in luxury as we left poverty (and my mom) behind in College Point. When we were with Dad, we didn't have to worry about the heater or air conditioner not working. But we always returned home to Queens to our grim apartment and our mother overstressed from the financial strain.

I wouldn't want to revisit that time—moving from apartment to apartment, barely being able to keep up with the basics—but the instability of our lives and the adversity we experienced would play an important role in what was to come.

THE REMAINS OF CHILDHOOD

I'm not blaming anyone for my situation. It just was what it was. I had the unique experience of living at opposite extremes throughout my childhood and teenage years. The disparity between lifestyles was shocking and surreal—the tale of two homes I will never forget. As a result, I vowed that when I grew up, I would never experience poverty, and if I ever got married and had kids, I would never allow them to suffer because of it either. Years later, when my company became successful, people would often ask what drove me to work so hard, and I believe it was the remains of this childhood experience that did it.

In fact, when I was a kid, I made a promise to myself to take care of my mom, which in 2009 I was able to fulfill. I bought her a new three-bedroom condo in Sun City, Florida, leased a new car for her, and took care of all the daily upkeep expenses. For the first time in years, she could live with a sense of normalcy—no worries about electricity or phone service, and a permanent roof over her head.

Mom taught Donna and me to honor, respect, and appreciate the little things—having a place to live, enjoying a good meal, and most importantly, spending time with one another. We were a trio of survivors. I learned that a house is just four walls and a ceiling, a material thing, merely a place to live. But a home is where you find love and a sense of connection to family. It's a spiritual place. It's what you make it.

It was traumatic for me when my parents divorced and I had to witness wealth but live in poverty. It was distressing to see my mother suffer financially and work so hard while coping with her own loneliness. But we got through it all. And when I think about it, moving back to Queens turned out to be a blessing in disguise. It fortified me for life. It gave me an appreciation for what was truly important and fulfilled my two primary needs: love and connection with others and the ability to grow through adversity.

"IT FORTIFIED ME FOR LIFE."

IGNORING THE PIZZA MAN PREDICTION

To bring in some extra money, I got a part-time job after school at a small pizza shop in College Point called Ernie's. The manager, Sam, was a middle-aged, sloppy mess of a man who wore eyeglasses as thick as Coke bottles and spent his time either sleeping on the bags of flour in the back of the shop or verbally abusing the help. He was a nightmare.

With a sneering laugh, he'd always tell me how I would "amount to nothing" as he compared me to my friend Andrew. "He is going to be somebody someday," said Sam with sick enjoyment, "but you're a loser." I shouldn't have cared what the creep said to me. But to a vulnerable teenager, his words were impossible to ignore, and they echoed in my mind for some time. But his underestimation and outright degradation of me only fueled my desire to prove him wrong.

I would find a way to make something out of myself, no matter what.

Although my grades were just average, I set my sights on attending more than just a so-so public high school in Queens. My first choice was Holy Cross, a private all-boys Roman Catholic high school in Flushing known for its legendary Knights athletic teams and a rich tradition of providing an outstanding education.

I took the entrance exam and was ecstatic when I was accepted. This was a major milestone in my life, and it symbolized the first time I took control over my own destiny and achieved something of significance. Up until then, I'd felt like a failure academically. But suddenly there was more than just a glimmer of optimism for my future. I wasn't going to be viewed as being one peg down from the guys who were better students than me. I wanted to associate with students who were excelling, and I wanted to pull myself up to their level.

It was an early lesson about the importance of choosing your peer group wisely—because, as I would learn later in life from peak performance coach Tony Robbins, who you spend time with is who you become. So when you step up to a higher standard and challenge yourself, you accomplish more.

THE POWER OF PROXIMITY

I had what could be called a high baseball IQ. In other words, I had an extensive knowledge of the game, and I had an unwavering hustle, but those weren't enough to get me on the very competitive Holy Cross baseball team. Playing baseball was not my destiny. *So what was?* I thought, as I continued to worry about my future and the financial conditions at home.

A pivotal moment came from a casual suggestion from my high school girlfriend, who worked part-time in the service department of Green Point Savings, the largest mortgage bank in New York. One night she told me there was a job opening at the bank. I quickly applied for it—and got it! As a seventeen-year-old high school student, with a background of service jobs, I had zero experience in banking. But Green Point didn't seem to care. Due to heavy customer demand for mortgages back in the mid-1980s, they were hiring kids like me who had no experience but had natural people skills. Within days I was working in the mortgage appraisal department—go figure. I put in tons of hours and learned everything I could. I was functioning in an adult world and excelling at it, talking with clients on the phone, processing their mortgages, and dealing with appraisals.

So why was this job so important? I picked up business etiquette: how to function in a corporate setting, how to conduct myself in meetings, how to be well-organized, how to understand the pecking order among 150 employees, and how to speak with clients on the phone. You can't learn all that from a book. You have to *be* there as an employee. It was priceless, hands-on experience that would give me an edge after I graduated from college and got my first full-time job. I would never again be intimidated by corporate culture, and I used all the skills I learned at Green Point when I later created my own company. Getting that job is key to my story because it illustrates how a position you're not even qualified for can teach you skills you'll use in another context, ultimately leading to your true purpose.

ST. JOHN'S: GETTING CLOSER TO MY DREAM

Life was really good: I had a driver's license, a girlfriend, and a part-time, after-school job. My view of myself was changing. I still felt broken after my parents' split and our move back to Queens. And I still was troubled by the disparity between our lifestyle and Dad's. But attending Holy Cross had helped me envision a better, more optimistic future.

And when the time was right, I started dreaming about attending St. John's University, in Jamaica, Queens, one of the largest Catholic schools in the country. I was motivated to apply there, primarily because of the school's stellar athletics. The St. John's Redmen (later changed to Red Storm) encompassed sixteen varsity athletic programs, including basketball, baseball, soccer, and football. Just as with Holy Cross, this was my dream, and I was driven to attain it. I almost didn't make it in since my SAT scores were dismal. In the end, I was accepted into St. John's, and thankfully, Dad paid for my college tuition. But instead of entering their bachelor's program, which had been my goal, I was admitted into their associate's degree curriculum, with a built-in contingency to convert to the bachelor's degree program if I proved myself.

I was happily thrust into campus culture at St. John's, with my focus on academics balanced with a passion for sports. In fact, a year into college, one of the senior bank tellers at Green Point told me he was putting together a company softball team and wondered if I'd be interested in joining it. His team was going to go up against the other banks in Queens. My eyes lit up. I flipped out and said, "Absolutely!" I'd never played slow-pitch softball in my life, but it sounded great to me. I had stopped playing baseball at sixteen when I didn't make the high school team. But the love of the game had never left me—and I was ready to go again.

The first day I took the field on the softball diamond playing first base, it was like being a kid all over again—except that this time, I was *excelling*. It was just an after-work league, but I was hooked, and I was getting closer to finding a "major" in life that would lead to success after college.

Next I found out about St. John's sports management program, which was one of the best in the U.S. It covered everything from the managerial aspects of sports management, sports marketing and psychology, stadium and arena management, and the techniques of effective coaching to working in the front office of professional sports teams.

With the global sports and recreation industries booming, the lure of St. John's was that they had a huge success rate in placing graduates with internships at pro teams such as the Yankees, Mets, Jets, Giants, Knicks, Nets, Rangers, or Islanders! I was like, "Oh my God, this is my calling; it's exactly right for me." It was a natural fit. I could combine my experience in business with my passion for sports.

So I was super excited about it when I shared the opportunity with my father, who said he'd run it by a few people. A few days later, Dad rejected the idea, telling me that if I majored in sports management,

I'd never get a job in professional sports and that I'd end up earning $17,000 a year as an elementary gym teacher.

I understood that from his standpoint, the safe bet—Plan B, so to speak—was for me to major in business management.

FORGET PLAN B

My advice to anyone reading this book is to forget Plan B! It irritates me when I see parents who are unsupportive of their children's desired college majors or other choices that genuinely reflect their true talent and passion. Over the years, I have known more than a few parents who have deterred their kid's talent to a "safer" college major. Do they really think their child is going to be successful in a job that holds no true appeal?

In short, Plan B is a cop-out. Having a fallback plan makes it too easy for you to give up on your true purpose in life, especially when you run into inevitable challenges or painful obstacles.

While we don't want to see our kids experience disappointment, much less failure, the hurt of such temporary setbacks pales in comparison to a lifetime of unfulfillment when you deter them from pursuing their dream.

Here I knew exactly what I wanted to do with my life, but I was seeking a stamp of approval from Dad and allowing his protective caution to deter me from what I felt was right for me. But I wasn't yet strong enough to stand up to his authority. I couldn't listen to my gut yet.

WHEN YOU FALL DOWN

- You learn to honor, respect, and appreciate the little things in life.
- You acknowledge that painful events of your life are blessings in disguise.
- You know that adversity makes you into the better person you will become.
- You realize who you spend time with is who you become: When you step up to a higher standard and challenge yourself, you accomplish more.
- You learn how a position you may not even be qualified for can teach you skills you'll use in another context, ultimately leading to your true purpose.
- You find out that Plan B is a cop-out: Don't give up your dream.

Chapter Three

CROSSROADS, WRONG TURNS, AND FEELING STUCK

After realizing I wasn't going to listen to my gut, I went to talk about my future with my favorite instructor, Professor Michael B. Walsh, who would turn out to be one of the most influential teachers of my life. A middle-aged, navy-suit-and-burgundy-tie kind of guy with an IBM-esque mentality, he had been a very successful businessman. He was fair, firm, often tough, and sometimes amusingly sarcastic. I loved his deadpan sense of humor. But I took him very seriously because I didn't want to *disappoint* him—a common thread in all my relationships with authority figures.

Just as I'd stated a hundred times before to Dad and myself, I told the professor, "I don't know which business specialty I should major in."

He said, "Of all your business classes, which one did you do the best in?"

I told him business management, his class, which was my favorite.

"Then *go* with it!" he answered. "And don't ever forget this: Nobody is ever *not* going to hire you based on a business sub-specialty. Do what you're most passionate about, and you'll do well." Yes, it was just commonsense advice, but I loved his blunt approach to business and to life.

In 1990, when I graduated with a bachelor's degree in business management from St. John's, I had a GPA of 3.75 in my business classes and an overall average of 3.0. Not bad, but where would relatively good grades take me? I was at a crossroads.

I kept thinking about my love of sports and how it could translate into an eventual job that utilized my business degree. That's when I started thinking I might go to law school, specifically to study sports law, and become a sports agent. I was so excited about it that I even took a prep course for the LSAT (Law School Admission Test) and busted my butt studying for months after school—scoring high enough to potentially get accepted to attend my first choice, San Diego's Cal Western School of Law, which specialized in sports and entertainment law.

I thought that Dad couldn't possibly be against *this* goal because having a law degree is a true asset. So I sat down to talk with him about it. "Dad, I think I want to go to law school to become a sports agent."

What did he say?

"First off, I'm not paying for it. You're on your own." That was OK with me. "Second, when you graduate from law school, you'll be $70,000 in debt, and lastly, there are too many lawyers out there anyway."

I was devastated because I felt that a career in sports management was truly my calling. But once again, Dad's disapproval did something to me. It felt like the final straw. I vowed that one day I was going to start making my own decisions about what was best for me.

With the idea of law school squashed, I started going to interviews for anything I could, from entry-level positions at JP Morgan to a little company that sold pagers (ah, yes . . . life before mobile phones) out of the World Trade Center. I was lost. At one point to make money, I sold home freezers (including a monthly meat delivery program!) door-to-door—all armed with my college degree.

MONEY, MONEY, MONEY

"Listen to me," said Dad. "Guys in medical sales are making six-figure salaries, and they've got great expense accounts, company cars, and health benefits. They call on me all the time." I always felt that medical sales was the only career my father ever approved of for me.

"I don't know if I can get you a job, but I can get you an *interview* for sure," he said. And sure enough, Dad found out about a job opening at a medical supplies distributor in Long Island City named Stepic Medical. After the first interview, it was a done deal. The owner said, "Kid, I'm going to give you a shot. I'll pay you $26,000 a year." I almost fell out of my chair. My friends who'd graduated St. John's were all getting entry-level salaries of $18,000 to $21,000.

Good-bye law school and a career in sports management. Dad's influence was huge, and in his mind, the expedient route to making money was the only way to go. And honestly, at this point in my life, I didn't have the strength to resist his will or a better offer on the table. And just like that, I started to cave. A great starting salary, benefits, and Dad's approval finished me off.

It wasn't long before I was racking up good sales numbers, converting my newfound physicians to our products, and rattling the competition. Within a few months, the owner called me into his office. "Kid, you're doing great; I'm going to give you a raise. You're now making $35,000 a year plus commission." Seriously? I couldn't believe it. This was insane. I still thought $26,000 was a lot of money. And now I heard that the bonus was probably going to be another $10,000 to $15,000. To me, $50,000 might just as well have been $1 million. Selling blood filters and cardiac cannulas (tubing) for open-heart surgery wasn't very compelling, but the money was great, so I told myself to just suck it up. I was also bartending on the weekends, having a blast serving up drinks at weddings and bar mitzvahs, making ninety dollars a party. It wasn't all bad. I was flying high and pulling in more money than I'd ever imagined. But my passion for sports was still alive.

U CAN'T TOUCH THIS

My sister Donna's boyfriend played in a local recreational softball league on Saturdays. One day, in passing, he asked if some of my friends and I would be interested in joining the team. After playing with the Green Point bank team on weeknights during college, this opportunity was just what I wanted. I was totally into it!

After that, it didn't take long before my college buddies suggested that I put a team together of our own—not only playing in it but *managing* it too. Frankly, I didn't want the administrative headaches: I didn't want the responsibility of collecting all the money from the guys to pay the league. I didn't want to create lineups (and risk upsetting my friends when I didn't put them early in the batting order). I didn't want to have to sit out my friends for somebody else, and I didn't want to manage the roster to ensure we had the best team on the field each week.

But this type of managerial decision came naturally to me from my days playing All-Star Baseball and Strat-O-Matic, so I reluctantly agreed to do it all—and I became the manager of the team. We called ourselves the Hammers, named for hip-hop's MC Hammer, who had a wildly popular song in the summer of 1990: "U Can't Touch This." (Hilarious and embarrassing.) A year later, we renamed ourselves the WiseGuys, which appropriately fit our personalities as a ragtag bunch of highly competitive, hot-headed Italians who often backed up our trash-talking mouths with our bat.

Although the league we played in was terribly disorganized, I was completely immersed in it. To get my teammates fired up, I wrote a humorous newsletter called *WiseGuy Weekly*; it was a tongue-in-cheek put-down of our athletic prowess after losing seven games in a row and filled with brutal sarcasm about the players.

I was a one-man frickin' newspaper, taking game photos and writing commentary—complete with an often R-rated quote of the week. The *WiseGuy Weekly* also included the schedule, my expanded tally of the standings, current season and career player statistics, historical team trivia—you name it. I was super efficient: We'd play our games on Sunday afternoons, and by evening, I'd be at home putting the paper together—writing the text, designing the layout, making photocopies at a nearby office supply store, and getting it in the mail the same night!

In fact, I was so into my softball work that I started working half-days at my real job. I'd blow the job off and go home to write articles for the *WiseGuy Weekly*. My life was revolving around softball. It was kind of crazy for me to risk losing my highly compensated career, and I did just enough to hold on to it.

YOUR PAST DOESN'T EQUAL YOUR FUTURE

I knew from my behavior regarding my job that I needed a change of direction in my life. I just didn't know where it was going to come from. One night in 1991, while channel surfing at 3:00 a.m., I came across an infomercial featuring a super tall guy with plastic-looking hair and big teeth. Dressed in a Hawaiian shirt, with palm trees swaying behind him in a Pacific Ocean locale, he was talking passionately about his program, which contained the *promise* to transform your life, allow you to tap into your fullest potential, and achieve success. The end result would be financial freedom and personal fulfillment—all the things I most wanted. It gave me *hope*. Maybe there *was* something more out there than a career in medical sales.

After watching that Tony Robbins infomercial, I purchased his *Personal Power* cassette tapes, and I listened to them in my car every day between visiting hospital clients. As Tony shared his personal stories on tape, I soon discovered that he came from a broken home, just like me. He grew up in dire financial circumstances. Ditto. He wasn't a great student and never even went to college! But in his twenties, he became a one-man industry, ultimately writing best sellers such as *Awaken the Giant Within*.

As much as I was intrigued by Tony's tapes, I had no idea how I could translate what I was hearing into making more money or finding my true purpose. I was so blind, even though it was staring me right in the face. Ever since I was a kid, I'd been fascinated with baseball: watching it, listening to it, keeping statistics, collecting cards, mastering board games—and managing the WiseGuys. Yet I couldn't see how I could turn it into a career in amateur sports. There was no such thing . . . no industry . . . no sector for making money that I knew of. I was blind to the possibilities.

"I WAS SO BLIND, EVEN THOUGH IT WAS STARING ME RIGHT IN THE FACE."

And then a light went on in my head: Tony kept talking about how your past doesn't equal your future. That was the biggest takeaway for me. Yes, I had some bruises—the trauma of a broken home, a father I saw as uncompromising, and financial deprivation as a kid. But after listening to Tony, I felt, for the first time, that maybe I could be in control of my own destiny.

So there I was at age twenty-four, hearing all about the *power of change* while hating my medical sales job. I can see now that just by buying those tapes I was already doing what others around me weren't willing to do—facing the concept of a transforming change. Rather than complaining about my life, I wanted to do something about it. I started reading anything I could about self-help and personal growth, including Tony's first book, *Unlimited Power.*

WHEN A MINUTE CAN CHANGE EVERYTHING

Tony taught me that we forget what power a single minute can hold—that an incisive decision can make change happen instantly. It doesn't have to take years. That was a concept that might have been heresy to Dad, but it was music to my ears.

Tony asserted that although some people will tell you it took ten years to change course, what they really mean is that it took ten years to get themselves to the point of being *fed up* enough to finally make a decision to change and then take *action*. The magical moment is when you hit an emotional *threshold*, and you have no choice but to walk through the *opening* to the unknown—the place where all change occurs.

How long does it take? According to Tony, *one minute*. It's in that minute that you can finally make a change to transform your career, or your health habits, or your romantic relationship, or your financial future. In a minute, you can make a friend or lose one. All this is the *power of a minute*.

Tony Robbins makes you want to change everything around you in that one minute. But, he warns, the enemy of the power of change is the power of procrastination, a common human action. Once we get *comfortable* in any job or routine, we find ourselves in the so-called Comfort Zone, a psychological state in which familiarity breeds inaction. Yes, you feel in control of your environment, safe and secure. But it's an intoxicating illusion that thwarts growth.

And that was my situation: I felt locked in golden handcuffs, earning enough money at medical sales to make it difficult for me to leave. But on top of that, I was concerned that I still couldn't see where I was going or how I was going to get there.

When was my minute coming?

WRONG TURNS

I kept listening to the Tony Robbins audiotapes, which were all about following your passion, the power of transformation, and creating abundance in life. All fired up, I got tempted about being my own boss, which led me to take a wrong turn.

To make a long story short, I got swindled into becoming a licensee of a company selling licensing partnerships that provided resources to high school students seeking college scholarships. I charged $15,000 on my credit card (dumb mistake!), investing it all in the marketing materials necessary for selling the program. Inevitably, the licensing company got shut down by the attorney general for fraud and went bankrupt—and with it went my entire investment. But I still had that balance on my credit card! Carrying that kind of debt, I had to work even harder at medical sales.

As a result of Dad's contacts and my track record at Stepic, I started getting attention from other medical sales companies. This led to my getting a new job at a much bigger company, Haemonetics, which offered a base salary of $40,000, plus a commission, estimated to be another $40,000. If I was going to hate medical sales, I might as well make more money at it. What else was I going to do? That was a question I still hadn't figured out, and my love of sports wasn't paying anything. So I viewed this job as a safe bet.

I was also becoming seduced by the lifestyles of the other medical sales reps, who were all making great money and building new homes. I didn't see any alternative. But as things turned out, I disliked the job at Haemonetics even more than the one I'd previously had at Stepic. The company's management made it difficult, if not impossible, for the sales team to collect commissions by constantly changing the bonus structure with impossible-to-hit numbers.

Admittedly, because my passion for softball continued, I spent as little time as possible at the new job, though I was not ready yet to give up the medical sales career. Instead, in 1994, thanks to a tip from a friend who had left Haemonetics, I got a job at a Colorado-based medical equipment manufacturer called COBE.

STUCK

Right from the start, I was inspired by the company culture, a much lighter atmosphere than I'd been used to. The management was friendly and the sales goals were reasonable, which allowed me more free time to expand my editions of the *WiseGuy Weekly* newsletter and play softball more often with the WiseGuys.

Throughout this period, I continued listening to Tony Robbins tapes, which got me thinking more and more about what I wanted out of life. I wanted to strike out and do something bold, and I began seriously contemplating the prospect of going into business for myself—starting an adult men's softball league. I even had a prospective name for the league: the ABA (Amateur Ballplayers Association) Softball League, which I envisioned as being the very best one on Long Island, though not necessarily the biggest. That was my dream.

In 1993, as I continued to play and manage the WiseGuys, I realized that the only thing stopping me from creating a softball league of my own was FEAR—in the words of one acronym, False Expectations Appearing Real. In spite of my dream, I still didn't have what it would take to try and compete against already established softball leagues on Long Island. So I stayed stuck, hemmed in by limiting beliefs, in frequent turmoil, thinking about how I might escape medical sales.

WHEN YOU COME TO A CROSSROADS, TAKE A WRONG TURN, OR FEEL STUCK

- Listen to your gut.
- Make your own decisions for your life.
- Keep your passion alive.
- Realize that your purpose may be staring you in the face.
- Instead of complaining about your life, embrace transformational change.
- Recognize that change occurs when you hit an emotional threshold.
- Understand that fear will try and stop you.
- Follow your dream—no matter where it goes, no matter what road you're on.

Chapter Four

EMBRACE YOUR FUTURE

I n 1994, equally stuck in my private life, I decided to take out a personal ad in a local community newspaper. After working long hours, experiencing a break-up, and not having a great view of marriage, I knew my mom and sister were right. I needed to get myself back into the dating world. The ad I wrote and placed in Long Island's *Yankee Trader* classifieds was written as if my dog were looking to set me up on a date. It turned out to be a winner.

SEEKING SWCF. I'm an adorable Labrador retriever who wants to set up my master with a special SWCF. He's a caring, SWCPMNS 26, intelligent, successful & attractive. Box #5317. ☎

SWCF = Single White Catholic Female
SWCPMNS = Single White Catholic Professional Male Non-Smoker

I also recorded a phone greeting that expounded a bit more about my interest in sports. It wasn't long before the messages started coming in. I went out on a few long dinner dates that were uniformly horrible. One girl, who apparently was very hungry, ordered practically every item on the menu, moaning after every bite. Another prospect talked the entire time about her ex-boyfriend and how I reminded her of him, even down to the fact that I ordered a Diet Coke like he used to. After that, I made a rule that I'd only meet someone for a simple cup of coffee.

A twenty-four-year-old woman named Nadine responded, and we immediately hit it off, talking on the phone for nearly twelve hours over the next two days. When we met in person on our first date, I was blown away. Holy cow! She was absolutely stunning—very slim with long curly dark hair, giant dark-brown eyes, and a gorgeous face. I felt incredibly awkward—like a cartoon character with my eyeballs popping out. Cupid had shot a direct hit into my heart. I had never seen anyone so beautiful, and I immediately fell in love.

We had a great deal in common: We were both from Queens, had parents who were divorced and single mothers who struggled due to financial circumstances. The hardships our moms faced resulted in both of us moving a dozen or so times during childhood. Our bond was instantaneous. From the first date on, we were inseparable. She was the first person I spoke to in the morning and the last one at night. In fact, from the time our courtship began, we immediately envisioned *marriage*, though I had always had an aversion to it and had sworn I wouldn't marry until I was thirty.

FORTY-NINE DAYS

But after a whirlwind romance of forty-nine days, we were engaged! Based on the deep connection we shared, the thought of marriage felt perfectly natural. We never doubted our feelings. But Dad did. When I called to tell him, he told me that I was ruining my life. "Why," he asked, "do you have to get engaged so *fast*? What's the rush? Why now? You've only known her a month and a half." Then he barked, "Man, "you're always running with your head down and shooting from the hip!"

That infuriated me. I *knew* what I felt for Nadine, and I *knew* what I was doing. Period. Nadine was unfazed. "I can understand how he felt," she said. "If your son said he was going to get married after a forty-nine-day courtship, you'd probably think he was making a poor decision, too."

Dad's initial criticisms of Nadine were reflective of what I believe was his worldview in general: You're not supposed to take any chances. But by that time, I realized that I was going to be a calculated risk-taker and that I was

> "BUT BY THAT TIME, I WAS REALIZING THAT I WAS GOING TO BE A CALCULATED RISK-TAKER, AND I WAS GOING TO TRUST MY VERY STRONG INTUITION."

going to trust my very strong intuition. Also by that time, I had drilled into my psyche that my past did not equal my future and that my destiny was going to be shaped by my decisions. I was going to live by that belief—whether or not Dad found a reason to validate my viewpoint.

MY NEW TEAM

Right from the start, Nadine totally supported my passion for softball. We were a team—and together we wanted to figure out how we could turn our passion into a full-time, profitable business. The leagues I was playing in were poorly run, from negligent league commissioners and last-minute or no schedules to incomplete or incorrect team standings. My vision was to change the way the game was played and raise its standards. That's when I hatched the idea of creating my own league—the ABA Softball League. It would communicate effectively with the teams and provide customized customer service.

As I thought about it, my efficiency would have to compensate for the scarcity of good fields available, since the best ones were monopolized by leagues that had been in existence for twenty years or more. The only way to beat them was to out-service them.

But when I told my friends I was going to start a softball league to raise the standards of the game I loved so much, they just laughed. Nobody thought I had a shot at succeeding—except for Nadine (and of course Mom, my sister, Donna, and my Uncle Larry, an avid softball player himself), who could quickly see how profitable a league could be. After all, every team had to pay a registration fee that averaged $1,000. So with three hundred local teams participating, that would be $300,000 in revenue!

In return, the league owner had to rent the fields from the county, buy the softballs, schedule the umpires, organize the schedules, pay for trophies, plus pay for insurance and marketing. Even with all these costs, they typically had an incredible 50 percent profit margin!

TWO STRIKES

But how was I going to do it? I was making about $80,000 a year at COBE. Doing the math, I figured I would need about 160 teams to replace that income. That was a lot of teams!

I called up a director of the Amateur Softball Association (ASA) and told him that I wanted to create a league of my own. Bruce dismissed me right off the bat. "Oh, no, you don't want to do that," he said condescendingly, treating me like a mere peasant. "You're *not* going to get any fields. Period. There are none available." He made it sound impossible to "get on the list," as he called it (to access fields). He said too many other leagues wanted them. He went on. "You've got to buy balls and trophies . . . get umpires . . . it's just not going to work." I thanked him for his time and hung up.

But I was not going to give up this time. I called the National Softball Association (NSA). The rep there said, "You're not at the bottom of the barrel as far as getting fields for your league—you are *below* the bottom." I took one more swing and approached the association I knew the least about—the United States Specialty Sports Association (USSSA). Marty Menningo, the New York State director, got on the phone. Every entrepreneur will face the kind of rejection I did on the first two phone calls, but sometimes you do get lucky and find someone who will look beyond their self-interest.

Marty's voice made him sound more like a loving grandfather than a ruthless softball competitor. His immediate reaction to my desire to run a softball league was, "Sure, why don't you come to my house to talk it over?" So I sat in his kitchen and told him how I wanted to start this league of my own and how Bruce, the ASA guy, told me all the reasons why it wouldn't work. "Of course, he was going to tell you that," said Marty. "Son, you called the guy who runs the largest softball league on Long Island. You were essentially telling him that you were going to be a new competitor!" But the long story short is that Marty did a great job of giving me a motivational pep talk and a new contact.

He concluded that the next step would be for me to reach out to the Long Island director of USSSA, Rick Marz—who would turn out to be the most influential person in my fledgling business. Rick, a schoolteacher by trade, freely shared with me a blueprint about how to run a league. Looking back at it now, if it hadn't been for Rick, I don't know if my business would've survived, much less thrived. He was an incredible mentor, navigating me through a countless number of pitfalls. As our relationship developed, he counseled me on the phone weekly, encouraging me even when things looked bleak.

A LEAGUE IS BORN!

I forged ahead, relentlessly going to every park and every school looking to get playing fields. I was like a machine. I knew how to present myself, and I communicated well with people. I used the same technique with the receptionist of a high school as I did with the chief of open-heart surgery at NYU Medical Center—a lot of schmoozing.

With relentless pursuit and follow up, I acquired a dozen fields scattered throughout western Suffolk County, Long Island. The quality of those fields may have been mediocre (at best), but it was a dozen more than anyone would have expected me to get. Then, to get players to register with us, I put an ad (double the size of every competitor's) for ABA in *Newsday*, a major Long Island newspaper.

I knew that we had to answer the phone *live*—unlike the other crappy leagues that never answered at all. So while I was at work, Nadine, who had only known me four months, offered to cover the calls. People started calling nonstop, and little by little, due to our tag-team approach of relentless follow-up, teams began registering for our unknown start-up league! It felt surreal, as though fate were guiding us. In just nine months from the time we began, we wound up getting a total of *fifty-three teams* for our very first year—thirty-five for the summer season and eighteen for the fall.

We were on to something!

DECLARING INDEPENDENCE

The opening of my first ABA season was a month away. But unfortunately, the tension between my father and me was skyrocketing. His consistently skeptical viewpoints combined with his negative judgments about ABA were pushing me toward the edge. At one point, he launched into a long lecture over the phone, telling me that I couldn't leave a lucrative career and that I was always *running with my head down*. He didn't mean this as a compliment; instead, it was a negative judgment, an assertion that I was too impulsive, that I wasn't looking where I was going when I made key life decisions—ones he didn't approve of.

I had tolerated his "Running with My Head Down" lecture for years, and when I got off that call, I was so enraged that I sat down at my computer and wrote him a ten-page, single-spaced letter. I totally blasted him, unleashing an accumulation of resentments and things I had never before said to him. The letter was my manifesto, my declaration of my independence, a cathartic action that released a multitude of emotions that had built up over the years. I let him have it.

I told him I had never felt supported by him and had always felt subjected to his negative judgments. He seemed to criticize everything I wanted to do—from my choice of majors, my wish to become a lawyer, my choices in girlfriends, my wife, and even the neighborhood of a home I purchased at one point.

He denigrated my choices and negated my passions, and I told him that he seemed only capable of giving me reasons why something *wouldn't* work, rather than giving an example of how it *could* work.

I immediately overnighted the letter to him, knowing that life would never be the same again. The next afternoon, to his credit, Dad called me in a quiet, calm voice. With little emotion, he asked if I could meet him on the boardwalk at Jones Beach. Our conversation was quite somber. There was no arguing, and we didn't discuss the letter in detail. We talked about our relationship, and he focused on defending himself—while also giving me a general apology.

Dad was who he was: conservative and happy sticking with the same full-time job for thirty years, no matter what. I was an emerging entrepreneur and becoming a calculated risk-taker.

OPENING DAY!

The day I'd been dreaming of finally arrived! It was Saturday, May 6, 1995, and the opening day of ABA's inaugural season was ready to begin at the East Islip Marina softball fields. It was a lopsided competition between two starkly contrasting competitors—one a team of athletic twentysomethings and the other an out-of-shape team of fortysomethings well past their prime. Nadine took action photos of it all while I schmoozed with my customers (aka the players).

It was so gratifying to see what we created!

Even though we provided our players with some of the worst-quality fields in Suffolk County, beggars couldn't be choosers. In spite of the fields, we charged each of thirty-five teams $800 to $900 per team, and we made sure they got their money's worth, which is a lesson in customer service for every start-up business.

- The teams wanted personalized communication, and they got it.

- Team members wanted a full twenty-six-game (thirteen-week) schedule, set in stone early, before the season began—not a piecemeal version of it one week at a time. We provided it.

- Team members wanted updated scores and standings. I used my experience on the *WiseGuy Weekly* newsletter and gave them just that.

I offered league management that surpassed the competition. Yes, we were small, we had less than adequate fields, but what made the difference was customer service! That was the first lesson ABA taught me. The end of our first year in business was capped off with an awards banquet for team members. Toward the end of the evening, a synchronous chant of "A-B-A! . . . A-B-A! . . . A-B-A!" erupted throughout the Polo Club Grill in Oakdale, Long Island.

In that moment, I knew I had found my *purpose* in life. This was what I was meant to do. I had the managerial ability, the love of the game, and the drive to create something spectacular! Soon enough, thanks to our outstanding customer service, teams stopped renewing with existing leagues and came over to ABA. This meant the other leagues were not renewing their best fields, so when competing leagues threw back their fields due to lack of demand, I grabbed them.

All this time, I had continued going to parks and schools hunting for new fields. Yes, it was hard keeping all the balls in the air, but by that time for me, it was second nature. I was the kid who had spent 10,000 hours mastering All-Star Baseball and Strat-O-Matic and then WiseGuy softball. So even though I had never run a softball league before, I knew exactly how to do it. Having the unflappable confidence that ABA was my mission in life, I was determined to shock my competitors and become a force to reckon with.

Building on the happy time of ABA's first season, Nadine and I went full steam ahead on our June wedding. The low-budget reception was paid for thanks to ABA's first season profits, and the ceremony at St. Francis de Sales Church in Patchogue was absolutely beautiful. It had special meaning to Nadine since all the members of her family had been baptized there.

HARD REALITIES

Nadine and I were excited about our future because we would be together, but the reality was that I was deep in debt due to my bad investment and in fact, because of the compounding interest charges, my credit card balance now exceeded $25,000—which might just as well have been a million dollars, since I had little savings. Adding to this debt were medical expenses for Nadine, who required thyroid surgery costing $60,000, making our premarital finances rather bleak.

In order to clear the accumulated debt, on the advice of our attorney, we made the painful decision to declare Chapter 7 bankruptcy. It was a clean sweep. While I still had the medical equipment sales job, we continued to live paycheck to paycheck due to the outrageous cost of living in New York, while also dealing with a lot of shame associated with being bankrupt. From that moment forward, we worked very hard to restore our credit and become financially responsible.

Then, in November 1995, just four months after the bankruptcy, my position was terminated at COBE. Just when we most needed that $80,000, it was gone.

In truth, since I had been so invested in getting ABA off the ground, I hadn't been giving the job anywhere near my full attention. Instead, every spare moment that I should have been canvassing hospitals was spent hammering the phones talking with potential new clients (teams), marketing for more registrations, meeting with parks and school officials in procuring better fields, or writing the league newsletter.

It was as if my entrepreneurial passion for sports management was killing off my day job, a Darwinian survival of the fittest. The job may have been my meal ticket, but Nadine and I believed that ABA was our golden ticket to much greater happiness and financial security.

NOTHING TO LOSE

After the bankruptcy and losing my job, what else was there to lose? Since Nadine and I had spent our entire lives growing up and working in Queens and Long Island, we both felt it was time to roll the dice and leave our roots behind to get a fresh start in another part of the country. We considered a move to Colorado or North Carolina, but Florida seemed like the best fit. The weather was great, and there were no state income taxes. It was time for action.

Our plan was to continue running ABA remotely from Florida. We were confident we could make it work since most of our time was spent on the phone rather than in person—managing the teams, the schedule, the fields, the umpires, and mishaps related to the weather. Predictably, every single member of our family was against the idea. "Why would you leave a perfectly good profession in medical sales to do this? It's crazy. It'll never work. You can't run a Long Island business from Florida. And why would you want to live there?"

True, ABA was in New York, but Nadine and I believed we'd make it work. In fact, we were confident that we could make it anywhere and that we could replicate ABA's success with leagues in Florida. Even if it didn't, we were young and could start over somewhere else. But how could I make the leap to Florida without full-time employment? I knew I wanted to be finished with medical sales forever, but I begrudgingly interviewed for yet *another* medical sales job on Long Island. ABA wasn't paying the bills yet, as the league had returned only $12,000 in profits the first year.

In record time, I was hired by Zimmer, an orthopedic surgical products company that specialized in hip and knee replacements, and offered a six-figure salary. I was now twenty-seven years old, and the job demanded all my time since I often got calls from trauma surgeons late at night when an emergency occurred. As usual, while the six-figure compensation was attractive, the stress and lack of fulfillment superseded any amount of money they could've paid me. Florida was still waiting.

After a few months on the job, I was sitting in my home office one spring night in 1996, updating ABA's summer league standings and watching Dwight Gooden of the Yankees pitch a no-hitter on TV. Throughout the evening, I was mentally distracted and obsessed with the idea of quitting my job and moving to Florida. To get myself to take that leap, I used a transformation technique I'd learned from Tony Robbins. It's called the Dickens Process and is based on the character Scrooge, who meets the Ghost of Christmas Future in *A Christmas Carol* by Charles Dickens. Scrooge is shown how he will be despised after his death if he keeps up his current behavior.

So that night, I pulled out a piece of paper and started writing all the pros and cons of staying in New York versus moving to Florida. On the plus side, staying in New York allowed me to remain close to Mom and Donna. I could also remain in a job that provided financial security, in a locale that was safe and familiar. On the negative side, with the forward momentum of ABA, in its second season with more registrations than ever, would it be worth potentially losing that business if I couldn't run it remotely? Was the gamble of starting all over in another state really worth it?

NO REGRETS

In the end, no matter what my insecurities, I concluded that there would be an even bigger opportunity in Florida. So why not take the chance and go for it?

By using the Dickens Process, I began to imagine how painful it would be to remain in the same rut, living the same old life, year after year. I kept thinking, *If I don't move, what will my life be like a year from now, or five years or ten years from now?* I imagined myself continuing to sell that medical equipment, year after year, pulled away from my passion for sports management, having to earn a salary to offset my mortgage and pay New York State's exorbitant cost of living along with its seemingly never-ending traffic and horrible winter weather. Depressing.

I painted such an ugly picture of my future about remaining in New York that by the end of the night, I made the decision that we were going to live a life of no regrets. I was no longer looking for reasons *not* to pursue my passion. And in the end, I made it more painful *not* to move than to move.

Nadine and I talked about it for hours on end. I told her we needed to let go of the security blanket that was keeping us locked in a comfort zone. We had one life, one chance. It was either do it now (before we had kids) or procrastinate, and move much, much later. I felt as if we would be kicking ourselves if we didn't make a move now. And as we talked it all through, our inner thoughts shifted from initial fear and ambivalence to hope and excited anticipation!

First, it seemed as if we were only living on Long Island by default—just because our ancestors had put us there! While we respected our family roots, we needed to uproot that tree and transplant it to a new location. We weren't going to be reckless. Ours would be a carefully thought-out, calculated risk, one that would not be deterred by fear.

We told our friends and family that a life change was no longer wishful thinking. Not a *should*, but a *must*. We were doing it. Predictably, few of our friends thought we had a shot at succeeding in Florida. Their rationales varied from stereotypical exaggerations such as "the Florida insects are this big" (using both hands) to noting that "alligators are so common they're walking across the street." But the real reason was that they didn't want us to leave *them*.

Ironically, the doubters and naysayers actually gave us the fuel we needed to solidify our decision to move. And in the end, did we have anything to lose? That's the thing about being in your twenties. It's a great time to be experimental and throw yourself at new opportunities, which is exactly what we did.

I started calling headhunters in Florida looking for (prepare yourself) *another* medical sales job—because ABA still wasn't providing a full-time income. That was it. I was done. Nadine and I were resolved, energized to embark on what would turn out to be one of the happiest chapters of our lives.

WHEN YOU DECIDE TO EMBRACE YOUR FUTURE

- You trust your intuition and become a calculated risk-taker.
- Your decisions shape your destiny.
- You don't wait for others to validate your viewpoints.
- You focus on how something *could* work instead of all the reasons why it won't.
- You use the Dickens Process to imagine how painful things will become in your future if you don't make the change you know you need to.
- You use the doubters and naysayers in your life as fuel to push forward.
- You have the confidence that you can start over and that you can make it anywhere.
- You let go of the insecurities, the golden handcuffs, and you go for it!

A SPECIAL NOTE TO PARENTS: Do your best to guide, support, and nourish your children as they try to embrace their future purpose. But don't force your priorities or dreams on them. We're all here with a mission in life and a destiny designed just for us.

PART TWO

Chapter Five

BE READY TO TRY SOMETHING ELSE

September 30, 1996, was moving day. But when that fateful day arrived, it was a bittersweet moment. We felt as if not only a chapter but an entire book of our lives was coming to a close. And—best of all—the unwritten sequel would be filled with unlimited possibilities! It wasn't just a move; it was a one-way ticket to a brand-new life! Whenever anyone doubted our new adventure, we repeated a mantra to ourselves: "If it doesn't work out, we'll try something else. . . . And if *that* doesn't work, we'll try something else."

That fall, we got settled in Brandon (a suburb east of Tampa). The business and motivational books I was reading had one theme that continually struck me: The real secret to success is not talent—but hunger! You've got to feel a burning desire within. It's the part of you that says: "I won't stop. I won't give up." It is determination fueled by creativity. You see it in the incredible stories of pioneers such as Walt Disney, Richard Branson, and the late Steve Jobs. They all had that level of hunger. I did too.

I wanted to create the largest amateur sports league in the country. Period. At this point, ABA was in the middle of its fall season, and we were managing to run it remotely. But I still needed a day job for a stable income and health benefits.

"I WANTED TO CREATE THE LARGEST AMATEUR SPORTS LEAGUE IN THE COUNTRY. PERIOD."

So once again, I went back into the medical field, this time as a sales rep for Pharmacia & Upjohn (now Pfizer). Career-wise, the perception might have been that I was moving backward—from medical equipment to pharmaceutical sales. But I didn't care. I knew I could do the job easily. All I had to do was call on eight to ten doctors a day in South Tampa. And because the territory was so small, and there was no traffic to contend with, I could do this in just a few hours.

From time to time, I had to fly up to Long Island for a few days to personally tend to ABA business, such as securing ball-field contracts with parks and recreation departments and schools or meeting with umpire groups. During those quick trips, I'd pack my schedule tight. From early morning until late afternoon, I was at full speed, going from one school or park administrator to another. In the evening, I'd scout out additional fields. It never felt like work, which is why I never got tired of doing it. I was totally driven by my determination to beat the competition at their own game—while unbeknownst to them, I was living 1,500 miles away!

In fact, other than two of the umpire assignors at USSSA, nobody knew we had moved. The optics would have been terrible—a league owner who wasn't around to supervise his own teams. For the next three years, I led a double life—coasting on my day job while running a business with a 1-800 phone number that enabled players to call me without knowing my actual location. Despite the stress of maintaining a façade, I thrived on it. The tension between the job and ABA both energized and exhausted me, and it fueled my ambition to accomplish even more. I never took either source of income for granted, always aware that I could lose both of them in a heartbeat. That thought gave me my edge.

I frequently wanted to quit Pharmacia & Upjohn, but I knew I couldn't walk away from the money. This time, it was for a very good reason: Nadine was pregnant!

In May 1998, our daughter Taylor-Marie was born. I planned to give her the kind of total security I had never experienced as a kid, so her birth was yet another reason for me to stay focused and determined to build ABA. Taylor-Marie was the center of our world, and I had a secure job and a thriving softball business in New York. Who could ask for anything more?

While I couldn't have been more content with my home life, I hated working for somebody else. Like any entrepreneur, I wanted to be independent—my own boss. I wanted to make my own rules rather than conform to somebody else's. I wanted to earn unlimited income as a result of my efforts, not a salary dictated by some corporation. I wanted to stop making somebody *else* rich. And I knew that ultimate career fulfillment would only come from running my own league.

> **"LIKE ANY ENTREPRENEUR, I WANTED TO BE INDEPENDENT— MY OWN BOSS."**

GAME ON!

Naturally, my initial goal was to expand the ABA Softball League into Florida, a market that was far less competitive than cutthroat New York.

As I pondered how to become profitable in Florida, I soaked up every-thing I could about amateur sports. I attended sports industry confer-ences, read all the journals, and studied the trends, analyzing why some owners maximized profits while others lost money. It was fascinating.

Regardless of their geographic location, the one thing that stood out was that all the league and tournament directors faced the same exact opportunities and challenges. Their success or failure was a prod-uct of *business acumen.* Some league owners were astute and masters of marketing; others were complete bozos, sloppy administratively and not very business-minded. I was hearing about the management experi-ences of owners from around the country, but any challenge I heard about was really a microcosm of my experi-ence on Long Island.

"I KNEW I COULD DO IT, BUT I JUST WASN'T SURE HOW."

I had been led to believe that it was impossibly difficult to start a league in another county or state—that I could never transplant my winning formula outside the scope of Long Island. But this was total B.S. If you knew how to run a league, a different geographical location was no obstacle at all. It was nothing more than an imaginary line you could easily cross with the right strategy. See-ing the lack of distinction was a pivotal moment for me, as it allowed me to broaden the scope of my ambition. I saw that going national was doable. To think otherwise was a limiting belief.

When it came to expanding my men's softball league business, I was determined to become a force in the amateur sports industry. I knew I could do it, but I just wasn't sure *how.* Not yet. But I sensed an incredible opportunity that nobody else had tuned in to. In early 1998 I stumbled upon an article about how the National Football League was launching a kids' flag football league as an outreach pro-gram designed to promote their brand.

While the NFL didn't provide any training or support on *how* to run a league, they did offer basic rule recommendations *and* the jerseys, flag belts, and footballs. It was nothing more than a vendor relationship. And although I had never envisioned starting a youth league before, I thought, *Why not?* True, I had a baby, a new home being built, and a full-time job, plus the challenge of running ABA remotely. How much more could I realistically manage?

I'm betting that many people would *not* have moved forward with another business, instead letting the opportunity go. But that wasn't me. If your purpose is calling, it doesn't wait for you to be good and ready to answer. What counts is what you *do* with the opportunity when that moment arrives. I wasn't going to take the safe route. Instead, I acted.

Playing it safe is a recipe for long-term failure. You're either growing or you're dying. There is no in-between. And I was hell-bent on being successful.

Not surprisingly, when Nadine and I shared our excitement about expanding into youth sports with our friends, they uniformly responded pessimistically. The consensus among the locals was that youth flag football "will never work because here in Florida kids play real football—tackle football. They're never going to play flag." If there is one thing I've learned, you can always count on people who don't know much (or dream much) to have a strong opinion and come up with reasons why something *won't* work. That was all I had to hear. Game on! It was time to quiet the doubters and naysayers. Again.

A GOLDEN OPPORTUNITY . . . AND REVENGE

In the summer of 1998, I did a little advertising in local newspapers, and I used yard signs to promote my youth flag football league. Every week I planted forty to fifty signs in the ground near elementary schools, outside fast-food restaurants, in residential neighborhoods, and near busy intersections. You couldn't drive around the Brandon area without seeing my signs.

My pitch, as I explained to the callers, was that the game was all about fun, safety, and convenience. "Good Sportsmanship" and "Everyone Plays" became our battle cries. And moms loved it! We registered one hundred kids with ease within a month. My first flag football season worked so well that I planned another one—and not just for the fall, but for the spring too. And would you believe that the following spring, I got *six hundred* kids to register? How did I do it? I went full throttle, balls-to-the-wall on marketing. I spent upward of $15,000 (using my profits from ABA) advertising on television, sports radio, yard signs, and billboards and newspaper ads. I also expanded our geographical reach into two additional residential family communities in the Tampa Bay area.

I did all this—why? Because I sensed that I was sitting on a golden opportunity nobody else had noticed yet—not even the NFL itself! In fact, I took full advantage of the early dot-com era and snatched up the domain name www.nflflagfootball.com. I had my brother-in-law, Rob, design and create a website for both my flag football league and ABA.

"THERE'S NO FREAKIN' WAY I'M GOING TO GIVE UP. I'M NOT GOING TO FAIL."

What was driving me to work sixteen or more hours a day on all of this? Truthfully, I felt that it was my *purpose* in life to make an impact in amateur sports. And there was something else too: an underlying motive of *revenge*. I was out to prove my competency, driven by slights from the past. To say that I was ambitious is an understatement. I was so driven that, even after a full day of pharmaceutical sales and ABA work, I stayed up until 3:00 or 4:00 a.m. working on the youth flag football business until I literally couldn't keep my eyes open.

With Nadine and Taylor-Marie sound asleep, I'd be in the spare bedroom (my home office) compiling team standings, schedules, and writing the newsletter. Once it was ready, I made hundreds of photocopies, cranking them through the folding machine and electronically stamping them for mailing. The room was like a printing factory, filled with the strong smell of burning ink from the small personal copier machine overheating from overuse! So yeah, it was difficult and hugely time-consuming to balance everything. But my vision to create a national sports organization was everything to me. I told myself, "There's no freakin' way I'm going to give up. I'm not going to fail."

TOO MUCH SUCCESS

By the end of 1999, with our baby, a new home, the demands of managing ABA remotely, my youth flag football league in Florida, and my full-time sales job, the responsibilities and pressures had continued to mount. As I wrote in my journal, "I am STRESSED OUT!" In fact, I cannot remember ever feeling so overwhelmed. I started to worry that I had bitten off more than I could chew.

When the second season of flag football drew a whopping six hundred player registrations, we weren't prepared for such an onslaught of new customers. Our marketing campaign had outperformed, and we had become victims of our own success by expanding into three locations—with no real employees! Many of our contracted referees were undependable college kids who sometimes didn't even bother showing up at games. They'd give me lame excuses, such as their car broke down or they overslept. I was consequently inundated with angry calls from coaches and parents screaming at me. It was my job to fix things, so I'd race to the field and start refereeing the games myself. It was overwhelming.

In the last week of the season, I was getting so many complaints that the phone wouldn't stop ringing. I finally yanked it out of the wall and smashed it down to the floor. "I'm never running flag football ever again!" I screamed to no one in particular. Feeling as overwhelmed as I did was partly due to the one-man band syndrome—believing I could do everything better than anyone else. This kind of perfectionism was driving me to control a company that was getting bigger than me.

My "side business" had grown into a monster: ABA had exploded from 35 to 122 teams—with roughly 2,500 people playing softball every Sunday. The sheer number of players exponentially increased the chances of one problem happening after another. I needed someone to help me manage and control it, and my unmanageable workload forced me to split my energies in too many directions. I felt trapped, almost at the breaking point.

The result was a combination of irritability and despair, and a seemingly never-ending feeling of being overwhelmed. I was on my *fifth* medical sales job, and I felt miserable because it seemed inevitable that this would be my permanent way of life. I was doing the same thing over and over again and getting the same results—the definition of insanity. Yet when I added up the figures, I concluded that I had to stick with pharmaceutical sales; even though ABA was now earning $60,000 per year, it wasn't stable enough income for me to rely solely on my self-employment. In spite of what appeared to be success, I still had the limiting belief that it was far too risky for me to rely on my own business—that true stability required that I work for a company. In retrospect, that is the most ridiculous thing I've ever heard. It's the exact reverse: When you're working for someone else, you can't control your own destiny, nor do you have unlimited income potential! As an employee, you are at their mercy and can be terminated at any time, for any reason.

"I FELT TRAPPED, ALMOST AT THE BREAKING POINT."

A DANGEROUS SLIP IN JUDGMENT

But in November 1999, rather than quit my full-time job, I started considering *selling* ABA instead! What was I thinking? It would have been insanity to give up a business that had more than tripled in revenue over five years. The fact that I was even thinking about it meant that I was coming dangerously close to giving up on my dream.

In start-up businesses, we often focus on how long we've been struggling, and we forget to acknowledge just how far we've come—and how close we are to a breakthrough. As I look back on it now, my judgment was impaired. The accumulated stress of all those years working into the wee hours, living a double life, and needing to provide a secure financial future for my family had taken me to this point of self-doubt.

I thought, *Maybe everyone was right about my ridiculous aspirations to succeed in amateur sports . . . after all, flag football is a nightmare, and ABA is so fragile . . . I could lose ABA in a heartbeat if my competitors ever found out that I lived in Florida . . . I should just be like everyone else and work my pharmaceutical job to the best of my ability.* I proposed my idea of selling ABA to a Long Island-based business broker. "What are you really selling? Anything tangible? All you've really got is a big mailing list. Maybe you could get $100,000 for it—at best."

Half of me felt incredibly guilty that I had even made that call to sell my baby, and the other half felt completely helpless at the broker's deflating response—as if all the work I'd done had been for nothing. Deep down, of course, I knew selling ABA was not the right answer. I had hit bottom emotionally, and I knew that I had to take massive action to pull myself out.

REACH OUT AND WALK ON HOT COALS

When entrepreneurs and non-entrepreneurs alike face such a stress point, they are wise to reach out to a mentor, a friend, a relative, or even a business coach. I could think of only one person.

In December 1999, after eight years of listening to Tony Robbins audiotapes, I finally took the plunge and registered for one of his live events—Unleash the Power Within—held at the Orlando Convention Center. At the time, it was a financial stretch for me to justify the cost of the event and a hotel for four days, so I split the hotel expenses with my brother-in-law, who was a New York City police officer and just as miserable in his career as I was in pharmaceutical sales.[2] We both wanted more out of life than just working for somebody else. I hoped the weekend would be a life-changer and give me the confidence to push through my fear about quitting my sales job once and for all.

Then, bigger than life, there he was! Tony Robbins, all six feet, seven inches of him, bounding onto the stage, roaring a "Welcome!" and high-fiving attendees from forty countries. I recognized his voice instantly, but his physical presence was something different. He was bigger than I imagined, and he spoke in blunt, graphic terms, which I found reassuring. He was human, very down-to-earth—a real person, which made me admire him even more. Although he was talking to thousands, I felt that he was speaking directly to me.

The seminar was all about unlocking your potential, the primal needs that drive every human being, the disabling power of fear and how to conquer it, and transforming your life. The lights in the huge room were turned down, and people got into "*state*," as Tony calls it. We began the Dickens Process. We connected with our deepest emotions about how our lives would be if we never changed the path we were on. I could hear people around me crying as they imagined their lives absent real change.

During the process, I thought of how painful it would be if I were never to achieve my true potential, if I bowed to the naysayers who doubted my ability. I thought of how my daughter would be impacted

---

2 Rob wanted to transition from law enforcement to website development. Soon after UPW, he and my sister relocated to Florida. He began working at a website start-up company in Sarasota, Florida, and later opened his own technology firm, XL Technologies.

by a dad who remained miserable staying in a job at any cost. The pain of it all was excruciating for me, and I said, "Hell, no!"

At the end of the first night, there was a firewalk, where people walked barefoot across coals heated to 1,200 degrees. Tony explained that for people to have a breakthrough, they have to do something they think is impossible. He uses firewalking as a metaphor, a test of a person's strength and courage.

And I did it!

By the end of the seminar, I made a commitment to myself that, once and for all, I was going to quit my dreaded medical sales career in April 2000, after my stock options became fully vested, and then I would rely solely on self-employment—my ABA Softball League business. I felt fortified by my resolve to quit Pharmacia & Upjohn, and I vowed to focus my full attention on ABA. I'm not suggesting that everyone take my resolve to quit a job as advice to blindly do the same. Every situation is different, and nobody can tell you when to pull the trigger. For me the pain of working for someone else was too excruciating. This time, for me, it would be sink or swim. It was exactly what I needed.

SINK OR SWIM

I began to work ABA as though my family's life depended on it. I was running with my head down, metaphorically racing from home plate to first, intending to win. The result was 100 percent growth. Incredibly, we doubled the number of ABA teams from 120 (in 1999) to 240 (in 2000), and we now were generating $248,000 annually! We earned a net income of $125,000. In a matter of months, I went from despair to making more money than I ever made in medical sales. ABA was thriving, and my stock options at Pharmacia & Upjohn finally vested, netting me $40,000. It was time to take the leap. I resigned the next day. It was the most amazing feeling.

It was a time of celebratory congratulations, and there wasn't a doubter or naysayer anywhere in sight. I'd already proven by doubling ABA's business in one year that we were on to something big. But I couldn't sit back and bask for very long. We had just doubled our business, but we still had no employees. We were now the largest adult men's softball league on Long Island, and I had surpassed Bruce's "You don't want to start a league" multi-decade reign in just six years. With the phone ringing off the hook, I now was in the midst of managing hundreds of teams, using a spare bedroom as my office, working day and night, seven days a week. As usual, I was doing everything myself. The pressure of running every aspect of a fast-growing business with no employees started causing me great anxiety.

What was I so nervous about? Just about *anything* I couldn't control, including umpires showing up late due to traffic, a field cancellation, even the weather! Anything and everything set me off.

As Michael Gerber writes in *The E Myth*: "Being the owner, sole proprietor, chief cook and bottle washer allows the owner to feel in control but leads to chaos. The business becomes a BOSS and burden, not providing the freedom you expected."[3]

Fortunately, counterbalancing the strain of running a business was our very happy family life. In September 2000, Nadine found out she was pregnant again. We had always wanted to be a family of four, so we were elated, though I admit that the responsibility of supporting our family only increased the pressure I continued to feel. Early that fall, I finally went to my doctor to address the stress, insomnia, and overwhelm I was experiencing. I told him I couldn't shut my mind off and couldn't get to sleep until the wee hours of the morning. He gave me a prescription for Xanax to "round out the corners" and lessen my anxiety. (Ironically, Xanax was manufactured by Pharmacia & Upjohn, one I

---

3   Michael E. Gerber, *The E-Myth Revisited: Why Most Small Businesses Don't Work and What to Do About It* (New York: Harper Collins, 1995).

used to sell to doctors.) And though I filled the prescription for it, the bottle sat in my desk drawer unused because I didn't want to become dependent on it. I knew that taking that pill wasn't going to solve my problems. It would only dull them temporarily.

And then it happened. One Sunday morning in November 2000, as the fall softball season was coming to an end, I finally reached the limit of my ability to deal with the stress. When an all-day rainout resulted in the cancellation of playoff games, the phones were ringing off the hook, and teams were freaking out, I reached for that bottle of Xanax. It was the first and last time I ever did.

GET SOME HELP

That was also the day I realized it was time to move ABA's official headquarters out of that spare bedroom and into a real office. If I didn't remove some of the burden from myself, I was going to wind up dependent on Xanax—which would signify that ABA was beyond my ability. That was *not* going to be the result of all my hard work.

I needed to rent an office and hire some staff. The thought of the responsibility and expense of that created its own anxiety, since whomever I hired would be depending on *me* for their livelihood. In the fall of 2000, a commercial real-estate agent showed me a 700-square-foot space in an industrial office park, perfect for a starter office.

My brother-in-law, Rob, who was a great listener and supporter, strongly encouraged me to hire a part-time bookkeeper. As I thought about it, I realized that my first hire had to be somebody who could manage our finances and tackle the day-to-day administrative office tasks, without necessarily having any knowledge of running a softball league.

The ad I placed in the *Tampa Tribune* yielded gold: Kim Armellino was a smart, enthusiastic, thirty-three-year-old married mother of two, with a bubbly personality and great positive energy. Boy, did I need her help! As she laughingly tells it:

Frank was an organized mess, in need of an extra pair of hands. With the business growing so fast, he was overwhelmed, doing everything himself and unable to focus fully on the administrative side of things. There were piles of statements all over the floor. I put everything into categories, then we got the bookkeeping software up and running, and found an accountant. What began as part-time work soon expanded into a full-time job.

Over the next sixteen years, Kim would truly become the heart and soul of our company, her value to us unrivaled. She would master ABA's financial management and the operation of every aspect of the business. Moreover, she had a wise intuition about things and would become for me a great sounding board as our company grew. In short, I had hit the employee lottery on the first try!

Within one year of opening the office and hiring Kim, the business nearly doubled yet again, going from $248,000 in 2000 to generating $423,000 in 2001. I couldn't have done it without Kim. We were booming. And so was our family—Nadine gave birth in May 2001 to our son, Frank Victor III (Frankie).

There are times in life when not making a change is absolutely the wrong thing to do. Sometimes you have to follow your intuition, your vision for a new future, and be bold, pushing past your fear and procrastination—which may involve moving, quitting, or even starting all over again.

Of course, I've known many people who have the exact opposite view and believe that progress is made in slow motion. They'll cautiously tell you, "If you don't know what to do, do *nothing*," which is really fear of making a decision.

I believe you should study the risk/reward ratio of any big decision. And then you just have to go with what you believe is the right option, and be ready to try something else to get where you need to be.

WHEN YOU ARE WILLING TO TRY SOMETHING ELSE

- You tell yourself, If things don't work out, try something else. And if that doesn't work try something else. You have nothing to lose.
- You acknowledge that the real secret to success is not talent—but hunger! You feel a burning desire that you can't ignore.
- You become a dedicated student of whatever you're interested in by going to conferences, reading industry journals, and soaking up everything you can to become an expert and get your edge.
- You recognize that when your purpose is calling you, it doesn't wait for you to be good and ready to answer.
- You realize that playing it safe in life is a recipe for long-term failure and unfulfillment.
- You refuse to fail because you refuse to give up.
- You know that when you're working for someone else, you can't control your own destiny, nor do you have unlimited income potential. You are at their mercy.
- You stop thinking about how long you've been struggling, and you acknowledge how far you have come.
- You hire someone to take the administrative burden from you so you can focus on growing the business.

Chapter Six

KILLING THE GOLDEN GOOSE

Back at the office, things were busier than ever. ABA was growing by leaps and bounds, with over 500 teams slated to play in the 2002 season. I hired three guys who were in their late twenties as additional full-time staff to help manage the operations of the league. Knowledgeable and passionate about softball, they were excited to be a part of our growing company, and they were also the masters of wit, jokes, and sarcasm. As a start-up, we didn't have a lot of rules or structure in our office culture, since I hated any uptight, buttoned-up protocol. I was a laid-back, easygoing boss. As a result we had fantastic camaraderie in the office, and our days were filled with nonstop laughs.

Going into the office each day was like walking into a comedy club. Kim, who has a great laugh, loved being an audience to all the mayhem. "We laughed a lot," she recalls, "so being in the office was a blast—more like hanging out with your friends than work." Despite the loose atmosphere, we worked hard and were very productive. In fact, I attribute part of our success to our relaxed team chemistry. You can't try to create that kind of rapport. It's either there or it isn't. And we had it. That's why those early years of building the business were among some of the happiest. With Kim and the guys lessening the burden of operational tasks, I was able to fully focus on the long-term strategy of the company—which had always been my strength. I viewed myself as more of an innovator, and I reveled in the creative process as opposed to the administrative role of a manager.

Our results were amazing. The business was now doing nearly $600,000 in annual revenue. I began asking myself, "How can we replicate the success of ABA *nationwide?*" I believed our unique system of running ABA could be repeated anywhere. I became obsessed with the idea of franchising ABA. It would allow me to play on a bigger stage and bring my vision of amateur sports to millions, making memories for adults and kids on a national scale.

A GAME CHANGER

In short, I wanted to be a game changer for the entire industry, and I was committed to reinventing the way amateur sports were organized. As I had observed, the industry was made up of league owners who were making great money but providing lousy service—not answering the phone, not creating schedules on time, not giving out awards, not having adequate umpires or referees, you name it. The bar was so low, and I was determined to raise it. In a practical sense, by franchising ABA, we could also offset the burden of all our administrative tasks related to running thousands of teams.

So after doing intense research on franchising, I came upon a well-known Chicago firm, iFranchise, run by Mark Siebert, who had successfully guided many entrepreneurs toward national expansion. After meeting with him, I was convinced he could do the same for me. True enough, within six months, Mark exceeded my expectations, delivering a complete structure for the franchise, the legal documents, and all the marketing materials focused on internet and magazine ads. Mark and I envisioned the ABA franchise offering franchisees the option to operate three adult or youth sports (choosing between flag football, baseball/softball, soccer, and basketball).

Because potential franchisees couldn't actually "see" the Long Island model (as going to one of our games wouldn't really give them any insight), they would have to rely on my pitch. I guess you could say I was selling them on a dream. I was prepared to tell them the full story of how I had started from nothing, but because I couldn't legally disclose how many teams there were or how much revenue I was making, I decided to fill our office with large acrylic trophies, one representing each year in ABA history. It was an effective way to proudly display the number of teams we had and the revenue milestones we were achieving.

"I GUESS YOU COULD SAY I WAS SELLING THEM ON A DREAM."

It may have been a bit self-glorifying, but it was a creative way of getting around the system.

As part of our standard franchisee benefits, I documented the entire protocol for running a league in a detailed, how-to operations manual, offered a training class, and provided ongoing telephone support.

If I was going to fulfill my vision of going national, the financial projections made it obvious that I would need to *sell* ABA to raise enough capital to reinvest in the national franchise effort. Yes, ABA was my baby, but franchising was a dream that required our full effort. As much as it had meant to me, I was going to have to let ABA go.

We needed hard cash to launch the franchise initiative. In fact, the $85,000 I had paid to hire iFranchise was just the beginning. For marketing, operational support, and working capital to survive while we built our franchise system, total start-up costs were going to be in the *$500,000* range. The not-so-distant pain Nadine and I had experienced during our bankruptcy made it clear that we were *not* about to take on a loan that would put us back into debt. Nor did we want to bring in any partner to fund us. So selling ABA was the logical way to go.

My father thought selling ABA to fund a national franchise was an unnecessary risk. "You can't kill the golden goose!" he told me emphatically. "I think you're making a big mistake. Perfection is the enemy of good, and you're ruining a great thing by selling ABA." But once Dad expressed his opposition to the plan, I was wholeheartedly determined to move forward. I'm not kidding. His opposition to selling was literally the sign to me that I was making the right decision in doing it.

Growth was calling out to me. I chose to franchise.

Change is *always* happening around you—whether you want it to or not. It's an inevitable law of nature. As the founder of McDonald's, Ray Kroc, once said: "When you're green you grow, when you're ripe, you rot." You can either be the catalyst for change or be its victim. It's not something you can stop. And it's totally your choice.

It was nerve-wracking to think about putting ABA up for sale and franchising an unknown concept. But I felt I was following my *purpose*—that everything I had ever done since I was a kid had led me to this point. That conviction left me with a quiet, calm confidence. I knew it was the right thing to do for our future.

I TO THE 9TH POWER

The first thing we needed to do was find a *name* for our national company, and I was obsessed with finding the right one. At the office, we put up giant sheets of paper on the walls and considered dozens of names. Among the finalists were *Ampro Sports Leagues* and *X-Factor Sports*. But neither of them hit the mark. While I theoretically wanted to be collaborative and get my staff involved in naming the company, it was slow going since there were too many conflicting opinions.

One late night in July 2002, I began writing down dozens of words that were symbolic of our company's mission. To my surprise, there were nine words that jumped off the page, all beginning with the letter "i": *innovative, imaginative, impassioned, inspirational, interactive, insightful, inclusive, instructional,* and *integrity-driven*. It all added up to i to the 9th power! Using this concept as a company name would be unique—giving us strong trademark protection. It was powerful, and I felt with absolute certainty that it was the DNA of our new business.

Next, I had to create a logo. I wanted it to be very Americana with a high-tech, edgy feel. I worked with a graphic designer who worked for my brother-in-law, and we came up with a concept incorporating red, white, blue, and silver.

The dark blue (used for the i9) was New York Yankee blue, representing tradition and integrity; the red (used for the word *Sports*) stood for passion; and the elliptical shape was Dallas Cowboys silver, which added a contemporary high-tech feel.

We were now ready for the final hurdle before we could launch i9 Sports. It was time to put ABA up for sale. In 2003, the company had blossomed to nearly eight hundred teams and was grossing $739,000 in annual revenue. I went to a Long Island-based broker who suggested that we put it on the market for $1 million. I was blown away by his recommendation. (Good thing I had refused to sell it for $100,000 four years earlier!)

Within a month, we had a buyer who offered me $900,000 in cash up front, plus a 7.5 percent ongoing royalty of the revenue for the next ten years in exchange for becoming franchisees of both adult and youth sports. In total, the deal turned out to be worth over $2 million. Not bad for a little fly-by-night softball league on Long Island that nobody believed could get off the ground—a company created by a guy with no connections on a shoestring budget.

After taxes and broker fees, I walked away with $550,000 of the $900,000 up-front money—a sum that felt like a billion dollars to me. It would instantly provide the working capital needed to launch i9 Sports. Sure, I would have to prove that i9 could be a real profit-making business opportunity in an industry predominately led by nonprofit organizations such as the YMCA, Little League, and the public parks and recreation departments. I would have to show that i9 Sports was different from everyone else because we were *not* run by volunteers; there were no burdens on the parents to do mandatory fund-raisers, or work the concessions stand, or sell popcorn and candy outside the local supermarket.

Our franchisees would operate the leagues full-time, and their goal would be to provide an outstanding customer experience. We would offer an alternative to the hypercompetitive, win-at-all-costs culture that pervaded most kids' sports leagues. We would offer families an experience that focused on *fun, safety*, and *convenience*. Toward this goal, practices and games would be scheduled on the *same* day. This was far more convenient for parents than having practices during the week and games on the weekend.

We would offer not only baseball and flag football, but also sports I'd never dealt with before—basketball, soccer, golf, volleyball, and hockey. Even though they were all quite different, in my mind, since I had a winning *system* of running an adult men's softball and youth flag football league, it didn't matter whether the ball was being kicked or thrown. Maybe I had only successfully operated my adult men's softball league on Long Island and my youth flag football in Tampa for a short stint. But from years of attending amateur sports industry conferences and talking to private sports-complex owners, I knew they all had the same administrative problems regardless of their geographical location. The regional differences were separated, in my mind, by an imaginary line that I could cross over. And as always, I referred back to the idea that I would not allow a *limiting belief* to stop me. The same problems exist everywhere, and I had a system for solving them. *What's the big deal?* I thought.

BUILDING THE PLANE ON THE WAY DOWN

It was now late 2003, and ready or not, it was time to roll! For an initial franchise fee of $18,500 (plus a 7.5 percent ongoing royalty), i9 Sports franchisees would be given the rights to operate three adult or youth sports in a protected territory. To manage their leagues, they'd be utilizing our detailed operating manual, marketing materials, a customized website, and proprietary software. They would also receive five days of classroom training at our office in Florida, as well as ongoing telephone and online support.

As the chairman of LinkedIn once said: "An entrepreneur is someone who jumps off a cliff and builds a plane on the way down." That's essentially what I was doing. I was now at the office day and night, once again running with my head down and obsessed with just one thing: selling franchises. There was no in-between. Everything was on the line. If we didn't get any sales, there was no company. Fortunately, from the get-go, phone calls and hundreds of online inquiries started pouring in. But I clearly didn't have an adequate marketing or operations system in place to support the franchisees' efforts.

With only royalty income from ABA, I worked feverishly to get i9 Sports off the ground, talking with potential franchisees day and night, seven days per week. As a result, my family life suffered, swallowed up by the endless list of phone calls to make and a bottomless to-do list.

In November 2003, I sold my first i9 franchise to a businessman in Tampa, quickly followed by another two sales, all based in Florida. I was overjoyed and a little nervous too. Why? Because two of the three franchisees intended to offer *youth* sports—not my specialty. In fact, our training manual should have changed content according to the youth or adult sports, but it didn't. Instead, one template served all, which was a big mistake, one that would soon come back to bite me. But for now, life was good. We were flush with cash—and filled with optimism.

I continued to sell more and more franchises to people from coast to coast, though my criteria for franchisees were admittedly not terribly high. Back then, if somebody loved sports, had a charismatic personality, communicated well, and had the funds, I sold them a franchise. In other words, pretty much everybody got the green light, even if they had a below-average credit score and little or no business acumen. I honestly couldn't make the distinction of who would be successful because I'd never sold franchises before. I had to go purely with my gut.

Only later did I realize that owning a business and loving sports were two separate things. Just because you knew the rules of football and were a diehard fan or even played the game professionally didn't mean you should own a football business. Unsuitable franchisees would fail because they neglected to execute the marketing strategy, manage their finances, or train their staff.

I didn't recognize this back then because I was so hell-bent on sales. Yet my throw-it-against-the-wall-to-see-if-it-sticks strategy seemed to be working. In fact, with a dozen or so new franchisees under our belt and a continuing influx of phone calls, I needed to hire more support staff—and fast.

But rather than delegating the search, as an entrepreneur should do whenever possible, I did it all myself. I understood the right business skill set needed for each position, but I overlooked the interpersonal skills factor. I started hiring all the wrong people.

FREE FALL

In the midst of staff chaos, the volume of business was so insane that we had far outgrown our small office space. I decided to buy a brand-new, stand-alone office, a 2,500-square-foot brick office building in Brandon. At this point in 2005, we had sold thirty-five franchises, many of them to people we would never approve today. Compounding the problem was a staff that wasn't supporting them very well.

Rightfully so, our franchisees were riled up and complaining that our system wasn't working for them and that they weren't making enough money, which, in turn, meant that our finances suffered too. In fact, unless the franchisees thrived, no royalties would flow our way. Instead, we found ourselves staying afloat by selling additional franchises. It was a downhill spiral that picked up steam as franchisees became increasingly restless.

It became apparent to me that the franchisees who bought my adult sports version were not having the success I had experienced with ABA, despite having my "proven formula" for success. It seemed as if my Long Island softball league was an anomaly, specific to the Northeast and not instantly repeatable across the country.

As if this weren't worrisome enough, our youth sports franchisees were operating with way too many inconsistencies. We were so focused on selling franchises to keep our head above water that enforcing standard operating procedures on our youth sports franchisees was the furthest thing from my mind. And when I tried to rein them in, the franchisee mantra was: "It's different in my area." Inconsistency was ruling the day. It was the *Wild West!*

In an effort to provide a consistent customer experience, I felt desperate to corral the franchisees, but it was a never-ending battle. They were often resistant to our direction, and I couldn't totally blame them for it. We had at least three problems: We had a staff that couldn't help the situation. We had split ourselves in two—both adult and kids' sports—but were using only one manual for businesses that couldn't have been more different. And we were offering too many different sports that weren't perfected.

The reality was that i9 was losing money head over heels because our overhead was too high. This was mostly due to employee salaries, marketing for franchise sales, and operating expenses. By the end of 2004, we had lost $350,000 and by 2005, we lost an additional $500,00. The company was in free fall, probably six months from shutting our doors. While I had sold ABA for a good sum, it became evident that i9 was not a proven system, and it had very inconsistent franchisee results, which is why it was now on life support. Everything I had built was in jeopardy. We'd lost over $800,000—every penny I'd made from the sale of ABA plus the revenue we generated from i9. Nadine and I had $50,000 left in the bank.

From the outside, friends, family, employees, and franchisees thought it was business as usual. But on the inside, the walls were crumbling. Inside my head, of course, I could hear the *I-told-you-sos* of all the people who had doubted my decision to sell the golden goose to go into the franchise business. But that just motivated me more. Nadine and I kept our company's financials a secret. Nobody knew the truth except Kim, who kept our books, dismal as they were. While most people would've been ready to quit, Kim still believed in our company. "It was a little scary watching the big account go down, but I never doubted that i9 was going to be successful. I had a blind faith in Frank." Nadine and I continued to have faith too.

NOTHING WAS GOING TO STOP ME

The operation of our business was severely broken—we had to face that fact. But we remained calm and confident that we were going to do whatever was necessary to turn it around, even when things looked quite bleak. I had the conviction with every fiber of my being that, in spite of what was happening, nothing was going to stop me this time.

When things get really tough, that's when you know your mettle is really being tested. At that point, if you have any doubt that what you're doing isn't worth fighting for, then you're toast. So, no matter how bad things got for us at i9, I continued to believe that I was destined to make a big impact in the amateur sports industry. And equally as important was my willingness to take massive action to solve our problems. We had come way too far to fail, and we were going to do anything it took to turn i9 around—and were going to do it swiftly.

WHEN YOU'VE CREATED A GOLDEN GOOSE

- Remember that team company chemistry and rapport are crucial to success.
- Know when it's time to focus on tasks that highlight your skills. If you are an innovator, find someone else to do operations or management.
- When you're ready to take your success and vision to the next level, consult a professional who has already done what you want to do.
- When growth calls out to you, prepare yourself to let go of the idea of your company as it once was. Don't let sentimental feelings get in the way of doing what's right for the business.
- Change is always happening around you—whether you want it or not. You can either be the catalyst for change or be its victim. It's totally your choice.
- Once you've committed to change, be ready to jump off the cliff and build the plane on the way down.
- Don't compromise your family life or your emotional well-being. Life is a balance.
- If things start to spin out of control, you must believe wholeheartedly in your cause and take massive action!

Chapter Seven

A LIFE OF NO REGRETS

Small businesses often need help—an outside perspective from skilled advisors, mentors, or paid consultants. Finding that right person is key. But first you have to be willing and receptive to the idea. It was important for me to shift gears away from total self-reliance to a coaching mentality, where I would have the willingness to take direction and feedback. The right person would possess long-term thinking, similar values, and empathy for where I was and where I wanted to be. So in September 2005, out of desperation to turn things around quickly, I attended a franchisor conference in Hollywood, Florida, hoping to learn anything I could to get us back on track.

The seminar's moderator, Joe Mathews, was the founder of the Franchise Performance Group and an expert in franchise sales and recruitment. His impressive résumé included leadership roles at Subway, Blimpie, MotoPhoto, and the Entrepreneur's Source franchise companies. He had been fully involved in Subway during its meteoric rise back in the 1990s.

After hearing Joe talk with such authority, I sprang into action and introduced myself to him. "Joe," I began, "I need your help. I'm going out of business fast!" He listened intently as I gave him the ugly truth: Our company was in dire financial straits, possibly only six months from collapse; we had an erratic management team; and dozens of failing franchisees had not amassed enough critical mass for us to survive on royalties.

Joe agreed to help, and two weeks later he flew back to Florida to meet Nadine and me for dinner in Brandon. Looking back on it now, I sometimes can't believe I remained so confident, considering the catastrophic downturn i9's fortune had taken. But I kept telling myself there was no way my dream was going to end like this.

Joe's opinion was that our business model was strong, but we were deficient in some fundamentals. We would need to revamp our operations manual, retrain the staff, tighten up franchisee support, and fine-tune every aspect of our operation—"blocking and tackling," as he described it. He offered to assemble an expert team to get i9 turned around. It sounded like the lifeline that Nadine and I needed. But the estimated cost of the consulting with Joe would be $35,000, leaving Nadine and me with $15,000 to our names. We left the restaurant wondering if we should take a chance on Joe when we had so little money left. But Nadine reminded me of the motto we followed when we contemplated moving away from New York: Live a life of no regrets. We do things right or we don't do them at all!

"LIVE A LIFE OF NO REGRETS. WE DO THINGS RIGHT OR WE DON'T DO THEM AT ALL!"

The next morning, I called Joe. "Let's do it!" And *that* decision turned my entire world around. On Joe's first day, he and his colleague Chris Brown came into the office to interview my ragtag group of employees. Yes, they had their hearts in the right place, but they were a motley crew, and their skill sets and emotional IQs needed work!

By the end of the day, Joe had an I-don't-even-know-where-to-begin look on his face. "You've got to get rid of all of these people except Kim and your salesman." Deep down, I knew he was absolutely on point. My employees were hurting the company more than helping. They needed to go. Over time, one by one, I fired them all, with no remorse because it was the right thing to do for the business and my franchisees.

Next Joe and I revamped the operations manual, turning it into a more organized "cookbook" for franchisees. We created a system called Countdown to Game Time—a step-by-step breakdown of everything a franchisee needed to do from day one to start and operate a league. It included all the specifics of organizing the leagues: my proprietary system for researching and getting fields; the equipment needed; the award programs, how to manage finances and marketing; and how to maintain a custom website.

Joe also told me I needed to hire a consultant that specialized in consumer marketing, someone who could better advise us on how i9 Sports youth franchisees could get kids registered for our leagues. "And I know the perfect guy for you," he said, touting a seasoned marketing executive named Brian Sanders, who had recently started doing consulting work after leaving his post as the chief marketing officer of a multibillion-dollar publicly traded direct-mail company, where he had led their six-hundred-person sales team. Brian's expertise was assessing a company's competitive position, crystallizing their unique value proposition, and creating "breakout" marketing strategies.

At Joe's suggestion, Brian flew down to Tampa. When he walked into our office, the forty-four-year-old looked like the epitome of success, conservatively dressed in a navy-blue suit, crisp white shirt, and frameless eyeglasses. Something about his clean-cut, calm demeanor was soothing to me. He reminded me of a younger version of Professor Walsh, my favorite instructor back at St. John's. My intuition was strong that he knew what he was talking about. As Brian remembers it:

When I first met Frank, he was very short-handed, with thirty-five franchisees who were all doing their own thing. The i9 customers were being given inconsistent sports experiences, since each franchisee experimented with different marketing tactics and ways to run the program. It was all trial and error, with no master blueprint. My job was to bring consistency and order to it.

A JEWEL OF A BUSINESS

By late fall of 2005, Brian had consulted with us for an eight-week assignment that included interviewing our franchisees to assess what was and wasn't working. He surveyed thousands of i9 customers and surmised that we weren't charging enough. Brian also emphasized that since three-quarters of all the parents who registered their kids were the moms, we needed to advertise wherever we could to reach them—direct mail postcards, online, retail shops, fast-food drive-through restaurants, pediatric doctor offices, and even daycare centers and preschools.

"As I got parents and franchise owners to talk to me," says Brian, "I collected lots of golden nuggets, connected the dots, and came up with a formula. One key point: In the i9 Sports model, instead of owning real estate, we rent or lease fields. But you've got to make that venue look like a *storefront*. Therefore, we needed to brand the field so people could see it was a celebration of kids in sports. Overall, it was as if Frank had all the pieces, but they just weren't yet sewn all together."

Once this basic marketing research was completed, Brian crystallized the "i9 experience," which consisted of a standard operating procedure with complete consumer branding on and off the field, including i9-branded canopies and cones, defined field dress and protocols, and the presentation of weekly sportsmanship values and awards for the kids. It was as if Brian redesigned our company's "storefront" in all its aspects.

Brian also created the first parental pledge (which has become a standard practice in the youth sports industry):

> *I, the parent or guardian of an i9 Sports team player, agree that the most important outcome of any game is for my child to have fun. My child needs my approval and support, regardless of what happens in the game. I will refrain from the use of negative or derogatory language aimed at the Officials, the Coaches, my child, or other players . . .*

I remember that as we wrapped up our work together, Brian said, "Frank, you don't know what a jewel of a business this is because you're so close to it. At i9, you're at the intersection of both providing meaning (by improving the lives of kids) while allowing franchise owners and staff to make a living doing it. That's rare."

Brian ended up being more than a paid consultant; he became a mentor to me, offering sage advice. From day one, what I particularly appreciated was that he was emotionally reassuring and professional at the same time. In fact, I half-jokingly said that I wanted to be *like* him when I grew up. And I feel that way to this day!

TURNAROUND TIME

The year 2006 was an incredible one for us. We were now selling franchises like crazy, at a rate of thirty-five per year.

And unlike 2004 and 2005—when i9 Sports had a cumulative loss of $850,000—we made $300,000 in net profit. The quality of franchisee candidates had much improved—vetted to more stringent standards, thanks in part to a new sales team.

In fact, franchises were now popping up everywhere, boosting i9's public profile nationwide, with no national competition yet breathing down our neck. From the very beginning, I often wondered how long it would be until we started seeing copycats. However, our four-year lead (and counting) provided the momentum we'd hoped for, and it gave us critical mass across the U.S.

In short, the turnaround of i9 was the result of a total team effort. Had Nadine and I not taken the risk (and assumed the expense) of swiftly bringing in Joe Mathews to recreate the operations manual and fire our pitiful staff, we would've failed; without Brian's masterful marketing plan and crystallization of the i9 customer experience, we wouldn't have lasted; and without Kim's dedication to keeping the office afloat, our ship would definitely have sunk!

As I thought about it later, having the courage to ask for help from others is an often-overlooked secret weapon in business success. You have to put down your pride and know when you need someone else's expertise outside your skill set.

The companies that make mistakes and act too slowly to implement change are often the ones that fail. It's the same reason why so many fledgling entrepreneurs flounder. When challenges arise, you can't over-ponder and avoid bold action. If your house is on fire, you've got to kick the door in and put that fire out with everything you've got!

During the start-up years of i9, we had problems with every aspect of our business: our *people*, our *product*, and our *process*. All three Ps were engulfed in flames, so to speak, yet we stayed calm and took the massive action required to fix them.

HARD DECISIONS

Notwithstanding our company's rebound, we soon had a new crisis on our hands. Up until then, the franchisees were marketing their flag football league as NFL Flag (just as I had done in the late '90s), *not* as i9 Sports. The theory was that nobody knew what i9 Sports was, while the NFL name drew all the moms and dads. But in January 2006, the

NFL abruptly announced that all NFL Flag Football leagues around the country would have to register their kids through a third-party website with whom they had a partnership—and if we wanted to continue using NFL's name, logo, and jerseys, we'd have to use their website too.

In essence, this would mean sharing our customer data with another company. I was totally opposed to the idea since that proprietary information was our most valuable asset.

If the NFL or the third-party website got access to i9's customer list, nothing would prevent them from competing with us directly by soliciting our customers. But our franchisees believed otherwise, arguing that they needed the NFL to lure and pitch to their customers. Should we give away our data so we could advertise as an NFL league—or should we take a leap of faith that our franchisees could market and generate business as an i9 Sports league? I had to choose a course of action that would inevitably seal the fate of the brand forever. I didn't have much time to ponder; a decision needed to be made over the weekend. I decided we would drop the reference to NFL altogether.

My belief was that our unique, aggressive marketing approach along with the quality of our programs was the reason we were successful, not the NFL name itself.

Just three months later, the results were in: We got more registrations marketing as an i9 Sports flag football league than we ever did under the NFL name!

In the end, I did what was right, not what was immediately popular.

In my opinion, this was the single greatest decision in the history of my company because it established i9 Sports as a brand. That alone opened doors for us to create and sell our own i9 Sports-branded merchandise, including logoed game balls, jerseys, and later, matching shorts.

EVERYONE IS A WINNER

In 2006, i9 faced another major challenge: an *identity* crisis related to our dual image as both a *youth* and *adult* sports league. While the youth leagues were growing at a rapid pace, adult sports continued to struggle. Franchisees offering adult sports were hollering, as they had from the start, that they weren't making enough money, and more than a few of them closed down. Others decided they wanted to switch over to kids' sports. From a marketing perspective, we were at a crossroads. What *was* i9 Sports? Like many companies growing by leaps and bounds, we couldn't offer multiple sports to both kids and adults while still maintaining standards and excelling equally in both markets.

Looking back, I can see that I was trying to be everything to everybody. I was hedging my bets, even though waffling in both directions was weighing us down. Despite making most of my money in adult sports and having limited personal success in youth, I knew in my heart that i9 was meant to be a youth sports franchise. And finally I decided that is what it would be—exclusively for kids.

Flexibility, rather than rigidity, is essential to following the market. The fluid approach keeps you from getting stuck, which in turn opens the door to greater possibilities. To accomplish it, though, you have to step out of your comfort zone.

Not only did I narrow our company down to youth sports, but I also eliminated volleyball, golf, and hockey, limiting it to strictly the sports we could commit to being the best: flag football, soccer, and basketball. Once we figured out that i9 was a kids' league, everything else fell into place. We rebranded ourselves, featuring only photos of kids on our website. We offered i9 Sports as "An Experience Beyond the Game," which we trademarked. Our messaging emphasized that i9 was much more than playing sports.

It was a sportsmanship experience—teaching life skills to kids. Each week, we emphasized a different *sportsmanship value* and gave a sportsmanship award to the player who exemplified it best. Values such as *listening, teamwork, enthusiasm,* and *courage* were traits fostered by all our coaches and our field staff. Starting back then and continuing today, we've had a lot of philosophical debate about giving kids awards. Should all kids get *participation trophies,* just for making an effort, even if they didn't win? Or should they only get an award if they rose above the competition and earned it?

As our business progressed, franchisees were telling us that they were getting complaints from masses of parents who wanted their kids to get trophies *regardless* of performance. Franchisees understandably didn't want to hurt their business by disappointing customers, and I certainly agreed with them. Personal opinion should never get in the way of what the consumer wants.

My personal view (which I've never shared publicly) was that players should be rewarded based on age-appropriateness. For example, I'm in favor of giving all kids ages three to six participation trophies (because quite honestly, you can't keep score for that age—nor are they even paying much attention to the game). However, for kids ages seven and up, I believe they should be rewarded for good sportsmanship and excellence only—and that means winning. My philosophy is that they need to learn how to win with grace and lose with dignity.

But I was not going to let my personal opinion get in the way of what was in the best interest of a private for-profit business. If the trend was that parents wanted their kids to receive awards, that's what we were going to do.

LONELY AT THE TOP

In September 2007, we reached a major milestone by selling our *one hundredth* franchise. We felt incredibly proud of this achievement since only 10 percent of all franchisors in the U.S. ever get to the one hundred mark! Amazingly, we did it in just under four years, and our locations were spread out from Hawaii to New York. At the office, we felt a positive momentum that was infectious. To celebrate our one hundredth, I took the entire staff and their spouses—a total of twenty-five people—out to a great steak dinner at one of Tampa's best restaurants.

But as the evening unfolded—and for the very first time ever—I felt oddly detached from my own team. When Nadine and I arrived and took our seats, it was apparent that my employees were avoiding our table. Clearly, I was no longer one of the guys. There was now something between us, and it was evident that my role in the office had morphed from buddy to boss. It was ironic that at the dinner meant to celebrate our company's achievement, I felt alienated from the very people who had helped me get to the top. I felt isolated and lonely, as if this was the price I had to pay for success.

Part of the issue was that i9 now had more employees than ever, and as the owner, I couldn't talk openly about every aspect of what was going on in the company. Mentally I had had to shift gears from the previous atmosphere of total camaraderie to one where I had to hold back when it was necessary. I simply couldn't confide everything that was going through my head because some of my decisions would ultimately impact people's jobs. I needed to create a very defined boundary line for my relationships with my employees, and while I was still friendly and receptive and kept my office door open as much as possible, I wasn't quite as interactive as before. I was no longer a substantial participant in the joking-around vibe at the office. It was like being dropped into an isolation chamber.

Kim recalls:

It's true that as the company grew, our relationship changed a lot. In the early days, it was more like friends working together, and I never thought of Frank as a boss. We were just co-workers. But when the business expanded, you could see Frank take a more authoritative role . . . and he would pull away.

It would have been helpful if I had been prepared for the lonely-at-the-top syndrome, but I wasn't. Leadership isolation is not something you generally read about in business books or college courses. Nobody prepares you for it. The loneliness that often comes with being a CEO may seem like a small price to pay for recognition, power, and success. But being isolated at the top can compromise your decision-making and leadership effectiveness. You need your senior team to push back when they disagree and challenge your thinking. Fortunately, I believe that I always made my team comfortable enough to challenge me and to share their views.

As I've since learned, every executive needs a sounding board who can act as an advisor and be trusted with confidential issues. This can be a group, or a retired mentor, or a coach, someone like a Tony Robbins. At this point in my career, I wasn't sure where to turn. While I would reach out to Brian or Joe by phone from time to time, I thought I needed a larger peer group of business owners on my own level to talk to—and I needed *friends*. Any socializing on my part had most certainly fallen by the wayside during the turbulent time of building my business. I guess I had a one-track mind when it came to thinking about i9. I'd even lost all contact with my high school and college buddies, including the WiseGuys who had been so important to me.

Instead, I spent virtually all my time at either the office or at home with Nadine and the kids. I had no recreation, no hobbies, and very few outside activities, other than going to baseball games and family getaways to Disney. From an emotional standpoint, I was getting most of my *connection* through employees at the office, even though that really wasn't working anymore. I was becoming more withdrawn and introverted.

But as so often happens for an entrepreneur, the rush of success had blocked out everything else.

IF YOU CAN SEE IT, YOU CAN GET IT

I finished off what had been a climactic year by attending a Tony Robbins seminar called Wealth Mastery, which promised to teach strategies that would take you beyond financial independence toward financial freedom. A large part of the work involved mastering your emotions and focusing on a series of goals that would become part of a master plan for success. As I listened to Tony, I could see that my style in business had been intuitive, a trial-and-error approach fueled by a consuming passion for sports. But if I wanted increased success, I would need the power of visualization.

Tony advised visualizing what you really want in your life, such as your top goals for the year, and focusing on those outcomes as if they had already happened. If you can see it, feel it, and imagine the thrill of it, you will achieve the same emotion as if you had actually experienced it. And that emotion will push you forward to your goal. Then Tony asked the attendees if the definition of wealth meant no worries, the means to do what you want when you want, and providing for your family while creating a legacy. Yes to all of it, I answered silently. I never wanted my family to experience the deprivation my mother, sister, and I had.

Tony said that anyone can build wealth if they have the right strategies and mindset. My aha moment came when I realized there is no *one* way or secret formula to making money—no silver bullet that applies to everyone. You could fulfill your financial dreams through business, real estate, stock market investing, or preferably a combination thereof. But what is a key part of building wealth is building a sense of joy and cultivating an attitude of gratitude. Wealth isn't just about what's in your bank account. It's a state of mind. As I listened, I was flooded with a sense of incredible thankfulness for Nadine, our two children, and a thriving business. I was so fortunate.

Overall, I was evolving in my complicated relationship to money. After years of feeling so incessantly concerned about money (and the lack thereof), I was finally ready to let go of the fear that had followed me my entire life. I'd always been a chronic worrier, fixated on things that were out of my control, including every aspect of the business— the employees, the franchisees, selling franchises, making payroll, our technology issues, expensive marketing campaigns, legal issues, and vendor fulfillment problems. In fact, I had begun to have *so* much to worry about that I couldn't even keep track of everything I was worried about! I finally realized that the only cure for my obsessive worrying was to just let all the worries go! I literally had so many problems that I couldn't even keep track of them all. It was problem overload. Rather than trying to deal with trying to solve all the concerns simultaneously, I needed to reduce my focus to strictly the ones that were actually in my control, and then address those in priority order knowing they would all be solved in the appropriate time.

I made a commitment to improve my life, while at the same time enjoying it more in the present rather than worrying about what *could* happen—or what had *already* happened.

I was more energized than ever, on an absolute high—but one that was not entirely natural.

A LIFE OF NO REGRETS

- When things get tough, don't be afraid to ask for help and be ready to tell the (ugly) truth about your situation.
- Be open to addressing your fundamentals and fine-tuning every aspect of your operation if the situation demands.
- Sometimes turning a bad situation around is just a matter of finding a few golden nuggets, connecting the dots, and coming up with a new formula.

continued

- A successful turnaround depends on strong team efforts and your willingness to take the risk (often financial) to get the help you need.
- Companies who survive and thrive don't *avoid* mistakes; they learn from them and quickly change direction.
- Flexibility is your friend. Step out of your comfort zone.
- Be ready to do what is right, not what is popular.
- Don't resign yourself to the loneliness that can come with being a CEO. Being isolated can compromise your decision-making and leadership effectiveness.
- Cultivate a sense of joy and an attitude of gratitude. Wealth isn't just what's in your bank account. It's a state of mind.
- Only focus on solving the problems that are truly in your control.

PART THREE

Chapter Eight

LIFE IN THE FAST LANE

From the time I left my pharmaceutical sales job in 2000, I never slowed down. I worked nonstop, worried nonstop, and let my social life go. I lived a life of pretty much constant stress. I sat behind my desk twelve to fifteen hours a day, eating high-calorie meals, mostly consisting of drive-through fast food and other snacks to get me through the day—empty calories just to fill me so I could get back to work.

I'd always had issues with my weight dating back to puberty. Due to our financial situation while growing up, I often ate junk or unhealthy food from the deli across the street from our apartment. This created poor eating habits and a false sense of comfort. By the time Nadine and I moved to Florida to restart our lives, I had lost forty pounds, and I kept the weight off for several years. But I started gaining all of it back again—and then some—after my son was born, during the time i9 was created. As the pressures mounted at the office, I put on more and more weight.

I wasn't exercising or even moving much—just sitting behind a desk morning, noon, and night, then going home and sitting on my butt. By 2006 my weight had ballooned by seventy-five pounds—from

170 to 245. The irony was that I was the CEO of a *sports* franchise com-pany. We were all about fitness. Yet the person running i9 was getting no exercise. Although our PR firm suggested TV interviews, I tried to avoid them because I was too embarrassed by my weight. I stuck to print or radio whenever possible.

In September 2006, while Nadine and I were in the process of remodeling our home, we went to a friend's lumberyard to pick out some crown molding. The owner, Roger, had always been quite overweight, but a much thinner version of him appeared that day. "I've lost a ton of weight!" he exclaimed proudly, telling us that he had a great doctor in South Tampa who provided him with appetite suppressants and weekly injections. I made an appointment with that doctor the very next day.

At the first appointment, the doctor immediately prescribed the appetite suppressant phendimetrazine, a drug similar to an amphet-amine. If you read the literature, it's only intended as a short-term supplement to diet and exercise. As the doctor explained it, it stim-ulates the central nervous system (nerves and brain), increases your heart rate and blood pressure, and decreases your appetite. He was right. It worked! After just one week, I had lost seven pounds. And every week after that, I could count on losing another three to four pounds, since I was no longer hungry. I was drinking a gallon of water per day, and I was soon exercising again with incredible vigor due to the hyperkinetic effect of the medication.

By Christmas 2006, I was down forty pounds, and by March, I had lost a total of seventy-five pounds—all in about six months. I naively continued taking the pills, under the doctor's supervision, and I was happy with how I looked. In fact, though, I was hooked on the pills, and there was no turning back. My excuse for taking them was that I'd gone to a doctor for weight management and they were pre-scribed to me as a safe route. Of course, I ignored the possibility that a doctor might extend the prescription for the pills since the drug was clearly indicated for *short-term use* only.

By the time my weight got down to 170, I obviously didn't need the diet pills anymore (and no doctor should have been prescribing them). But every time I stopped taking them, I started gaining the weight back. Without the pills, I was like a superhero without his powers, my energy depleted, so I'd go back to the doctor's office to get another prescription. It was a vicious cycle. And I was caught in it.

ESPIONAGE. *REALLY?*

Moving into 2008, i9 Sports was running on all cylinders, functioning at peak level with profits soaring, with a full-time staff of ten and growing. What had begun as a modest operation with two employees squeezed into a 700-square-foot office had transformed into a company that was quickly busting out of its 2,500-square-foot office space, so we purchased an additional office building across the street in the same office park. It had been a remarkable turnaround.

We were also earning numerous industry awards and accolades in newspapers and magazines. *Entrepreneur* and *Inc.* both placed us as one of the top franchisors and among the fastest growing privately owned companies in America, respectively. *Franchise Business Review* named us Franchise of the Year, a distinction based on a national survey of satisfied franchisees. Locally, in Brandon, Florida, the chamber of commerce gave us the Small Business of the Year award. We were on a roll, frequently up for an award and winning it!

As an added bonus, there was *still* no competitor breathing down our neck. In fact, from the time we started franchising in 2003 until 2008, I was amazed that we had never had any direct franchise competition in the youth sports league market.

Thanks to the positive PR and internet ads, our franchise sales leads continued to pour in by phone and online. And because my two main sales reps could no longer handle the overflow, we decided to add a third. He was thirty-five years old, engaging, and charismatic.

But to my surprise, after four months of attempting to sell franchises, he wasn't closing *any* deals. Despite his generous base salary, he asked me for a $5,000 advance against future sales commissions that were nowhere in sight. When I declined his request, he avoided me and everyone else for the next week, mostly staying in his office with the door closed. He never made eye contact. I assumed he was ashamed of his poor sales performance.

A week later, I was driving home from dinner with Nadine, and we stopped off at the office to use the restroom. When we entered the office, there he was along with his wife (whom we'd met only once before), hurrying out of a hallway, looking quite nervous. Like a deer in the headlights, he stammered that he had stopped off at the office to check his voicemail. Peculiar.

Later the same week, he resigned with no notice. A few months later, we got a postcard in the mail at home from his new company. The promotional card he was using was identical to the direct-mail piece that Brian had designed for i9 years earlier. In fact, the guy even forgot to Photoshop out the i9 Sports logo from the players' uniforms! Idiot.

It all made sense now. The new rep wasn't selling franchises because he was too busy stealing our proprietary manual and plotting to start a competing franchise of his own. We were absolutely livid! We felt violated, betrayed, and downright disappointed that we gave someone a job, he didn't produce any results whatsoever, and then he freely stole from us. To make a long story short, we sued him for both trademark infringement and the theft of the operations manual (which he returned through his attorney).

There were some lessons for us from this espionage. First off, we needed a better non-compete agreement to effectively protect our proprietary information from employees. Second, and more importantly, I realized that while anybody can copy your system, they can't steal your company culture, especially when they don't know *why* you do *what* you do. I wasn't too worried about this guy competing with us, because he had no strategic vision for the business like we did. The only thing he had was a copycat postcard and a lust for money.

WHY YOU DO IT

Despite the espionage crisis, I was feeling energized and drawing inspiration from reading anything I could about the art of entrepreneurship, including a new book, *Start with Why: How Great Leaders Inspire Everyone to Take Action.*

The author, Simon Sinek, a British-American motivational speaker and marketing consultant, wrote that there are two ways to influence human behavior: You can *manipulate* it, or you can *inspire* it. So while some companies sell their product through manipulation, such as *Buy One, Get One Free*, others do it via the Power of Why. Sinek says people don't buy *what* you do; they buy *why* you do it. What any successful company ultimately must do is create its raving fans. Giants such as Apple, Southwest Airlines, and Amazon had all done it—and I drew inspiration from their examples, aiming, in a much smaller way, to create a youth sports program that would make a real difference.

"INSPIRE OTHERS: THAT WAS MY GOAL."

I was fascinated to learn more about this Power of Why and wanted to associate myself with a peer group of fellow entrepreneurs facing the same kind of company issues as i9. I became a member of the Entrepreneurs Organization (EO) and took a trip to Boston in July 2008 to attend one of their national conferences. The highlight of the Boston seminar was hearing Simon Sinek speak in person:

> *Why do you get up in the morning? Why does your organization exist? When you think, act, and communicate starting with* Why, *you can inspire others.*

Inspire others: That was my goal. And it inspired me to create i9's mission statement: *Helping Kids Succeed in Life through Sports*. It's used in all our promotional materials and on our website. As we explained it to parents, team sports were one of the best ways to help children become physically and emotionally fit. Kids could develop life skills and a healthy lifestyle and boost self-esteem. And to avoid parental over-involvement, we stressed the element of *fun*, not competition. I remembered all too well those dads from my own Little League days who were ferociously hypercompetitive for their sons.

Everything considered, our pitch was a winning one, setting i9 on an unstoppable upward trajectory—until a few months later, when we were brought back to earth by the stock market crash of September 29th. The Dow Jones Industrial Average fell 777 points, the largest point drop in any single day in history up to that point. Unemployment was at 6 to 7 percent, with talk of it possibly rising to 10 percent. The real estate market had plummeted, with foreclosures running rampant due to greedy Wall Street investors and banks giving away subprime-rate adjustable mortgages to people who couldn't afford a mortgage once the rate went up. The Dow then continued falling, from 10,300 to 8,000 points in a matter of a few weeks, with talk that it might bottom out at 5,500.

HOW YOU CONTINUE TO DO IT

How could this be? It seemed as though everything was great one day and then Armageddon the next. With 401(k)s decimated and people losing their jobs, our franchisees were obviously incredibly nervous. Would parents still have the money to register their kids to play in i9 programs? Would people still buy franchises? As the leader of our company, I knew it was my job to remain calm and in charge, but this was the first time that I had ever dealt with economic forces out of my control.

At i9, to steady everyone, our message to franchisees was that we were choosing *not* to participate in the recession. We would take responsibility for our own results. So rather than blaming the recession on whomever might be the president of the United States or some government policy, I—unlike so many others—believed that our company's success or failure was based on our own decisions and execution of initiatives or lack thereof. *We* would be in control of our destiny. We focused on the profitability of existing franchisees more than ever.

Incredibly, from a consumer standpoint, i9 was like Teflon to the recession! Moms and dads continued to register at double-digit growth, and because we had about 110 franchisees in our system, we had enough critical mass in royalties to more than just survive. While the jury was still out about whether we would continue to sell franchises at a record clip, our revenues were soaring for the time being, which kept our franchisees happy and me confident that we would come out of the recession stronger than we had gone into it.

FIRST-RESPONDER-IN-CHIEF

By late fall 2008, with all that we'd accomplished, I came to realize that I could no longer take on every executive role in our company. The complexity of i9 had gotten way too big for one person to do so many roles. We had eclipsed one hundred franchises nationwide, and we had done it with a relatively small staff, no financial backing or outside investors, and no previous franchise experience. But the burdens of running the company were mounting.

- I now had about a dozen employees.

- I had one hundred-plus franchisees who relied on me to continually provide them with "a new shiny object," whether it was new software, new products, or improved ongoing customer support.

- As the face of i9 Sports, I was giving interviews on TV, radio, and in print while ensuring that I kept i9 out of any public relations crisis.

- As the CEO, I was the chief strategist overseeing over 100,000 customers in five hundred communities.

- As the president and COO, I was ultimately responsible for maximizing company profits by overseeing all day-to-day operations, including budget approval and tax planning, technology updates, testing new products and services, and participating in continuing education.

In short, my job title could've been First-Responder-in-Chief, because I was constantly in emergency mode, triaging and putting out company fires. Had I not loved the business as much as I did, I never would have lasted as long as I did. But once I recognized that I was spending too much time just trying to keep my head above water, I knew I needed a leader to take some of the burden off me. Ironically, I was browsing *Franchise Times* magazine when I came across an article about Brian Scudamore, the founder and CEO of 1-800-GOT-JUNK, the world's largest junk removal company.

Since we were both founders of fast-growing franchise companies, and members of the Entrepreneurs Organization (EO) and International Franchise Association (IFA), I was inspired to reach out to him, especially after I heard that he had hired a COO for his *own* company.

"When did you know you needed to do that?" I asked him in a phone chat.

"Frank, I'll just tell you this, you're going to know when the time is right. You'll feel it the moment you realize that your company is bigger than you!"

I said, "Yes, that's exactly where I am. The business is bigger than me, and the company needs something I can't give it. I'm the creator, more of the visionary, not great as an administrator executing the plans of operations." That's when I decided I needed to hire a president for i9.

So, while attending the Franchise Leadership Conference in October 2008, I started putting out feelers throughout the network of people in the industry, alerting them that I was looking for a president and COO to run the company. A few days after I got back home, there was a voicemail from my friend and mentor Brian Sanders, who had consulted with me three years earlier, crystallizing the i9 customer experience.

"I heard you're looking for a president of your company."

"Yeah, you know anybody?"

"*I* might be interested in throwing my hat into the ring."

As I drove home that night, I remember thinking to myself, *The search is over before it even really began.* Brian would be perfect, though in light of his impressive background, I never thought he'd be willing to move to Florida (especially since he and his wife had just completed building a new home in Connecticut a year earlier).

But within a week, Brian flew down to meet with me.

On the first night of his visit over dinner, ideas were flying back and forth across the table like a game of Ping-Pong. It was electric. We were both energized about the opportunity and totally clicked, just like we had when we first met back in 2005. Brian had vast corporate experience (including his time as chief marketing officer for Advo, the leader in direct mail, as well as VP at Maybelline Cosmetics and Sola Barnes Hind contact lenses). To accomplish all this, he obviously had great people skills, and he was the most polished and professional executive I'd ever met, radiating integrity to the nth degree.

I told him, "There is no way I can actually afford to pay you what you're worth, but I hope to do it one day!"

He just laughed and said, "Frank, I'm in a different place in my life right now. I'm doing this because I absolutely believe in i9. I love what this company stands for. And I want to do this."

Just a few weeks later, on December 1, 2008, Brian moved to Tampa and became our new president and COO, leading i9's day-to-day operations. In terms of managerial skills, we were yin and yang—opposite personalities that were highly complementary, perfectly balancing one another. I was the one with the impulsive energy, the passion to map out the big-picture goals for i9; Brian was methodical, someone who could calmly manage and execute a plan super efficiently. In that way, he took a lot of weight off my shoulders by focusing on the day-to-day details of i9.

As Brian tells it:

> *Since I was walking into a small business to work for a very hands-on founder, I wondered how much he would be willing to let go and trust. But he did! He gave me a lot of respect, allowed me to step into the administrative role, and we were very well aligned. Frank was more entrepreneurial, but I was able to bring structure and process. I can't recall a time where we vehemently disagreed on anything.*

Of course, if a problem did arise, we both rolled up our sleeves and became true partners. And neither one of us had an ego issue about our roles. So, while Brian quickly became the perfect president and COO for i9, leading the employees and communicating with the franchisees seamlessly, I was able to be the CEO and do what I do best—innovate and develop strategy—while also spending more time with my family.

"At the time I was hired," Brian adds, "*everyone* was reporting to Frank. He was worn out and just tired of it. That changed immediately, with most direct reports then coming to me. This allowed Frank to both take an extended hiatus to recover and enjoy his family, while I forged my own relationships with the existing home office team."

MY DATE WITH DESTINY

Just five months earlier, I had been intrigued by Simon Sinek's *Why We Do What We Do* philosophy. And now it was time for me to look into the mirror and ask *myself* that same question. In December 2008, I attended Date with Destiny, my fifth Tony Robbins event, and the longest one he offers—a weeklong marathon.

The event was a fifteen-hour-per-day deep dive into every aspect of our psyche. The goal was to figure out what made us tick and how our decisions affected our destinies. All of it would lead to answering the question, *Why do you do what you do?* Our mission was to redesign our lives to create what we most desired.

Coming into the event, I believed my "story" was about equating my self-worth with *achievement* and defying the odds I had faced as a boy when I felt rejected, inadequate, and underestimated. As I matured, I believed my story was all about *me* being or feeling *significant* in the world, being seen as *valuable* because of what I had *accomplished*. In fact, deep down, I felt that I would only be loved and respected *because* of my accolades. And finally, I believed that if I didn't succeed, I would lose the love I wanted and needed.

It quickly dawned on me that my intense need for *significance* in business, which I defined as a need for power and admiration, had cost me the ability to maximize closeness in personal relationships. I often held back, fearful that I would not receive the love I wanted, especially if I weren't significant *enough*. I also understood that my need for *certainty* had limited my success because of my need to control everything! Up until I'd hired Brian, I had lived by the motto, "If I want it done right, I've got to do it myself" (except when it came to Kim). Talk about significance and certainty all wound up together!

As Tony pointed out, most people want *love and connection*, but they settle for *significance* instead. That's exactly what I was doing. My false belief was that I was only worthy of love as long as I was successful in business. I was already aware of some of these beliefs, but the emotional impact of those fifteen-hour days was driving the points home for me in a new, intensified way, and I began to realize that I needed to be more loving, more accepting, and more forgiving—of myself and others. I always demanded more from myself than anyone else ever did, but I wasn't very forgiving if I disappointed myself by not getting results. I knew then that I would need to be more empathetic to everyone's human needs and the necessity to express pain, heal it, and move beyond it.

GRATITUDE

Another monumental breakthrough occurred on day four when Tony focused on consciously choosing your values in life and prioritizing them. He stressed the difference between *knowing* your values and consciously *choosing* your values and prioritizing them in a new sequence.

As I thought about it, it became so obvious to me that gratitude should be my number one and most important value. Don't get me wrong. I don't think I was ever an ungrateful person, but gratitude just wasn't something I consciously cultivated—much less was it the driving force in my life. But as I heard Tony talk more about his own deep appreciation for his good fortune, I saw that gratitude is a crucial component of a positive mindset. It gives you an instant feeling of well-being. It makes you feel happier and more satisfied in all areas of your life. And it reminds you to focus on all the good qualities of the people in your life and on the things you already have.

Tony also talked about each of us creating a *compelling future*, about finding something that gives your

> "ALL THESE THOUGHTS COLLIDED IN A FLASH, AND I REALIZED THAT THE BUSINESS I CREATED WAS NEVER ABOUT ME."

life meaning and drives you with a sense of purpose toward your goals, but also allows you to give something back to life. He asked whether we had visions that were strong enough to allow us to push forward through the challenges of life regardless of the pain we would meet. As I sat there listening intently, I felt as if my brain was being rewired. No longer was I driven so completely by the need for significance through financial success. Instead, my primary needs had switched to love, connection, and contribution. All these thoughts collided in a flash, and I realized that the business I created was never about me.

Yes, in the beginning, like most entrepreneurs, I was self-absorbed—since my identity was completely intertwined with the business. I told myself, "You *are* the Business. The Business is *you!*" But this distorted viewpoint amounted to the *limiting belief* that i9 and I were one and the same—that my value in life was in direct proportion to the success I achieved. This was both a blessing and a curse.

When i9 was doing well, I felt great about everything in my life. However, whenever the business had a crisis, my whole world suffered. It was all or nothing at all—my business dictated my happiness.

Sitting in that seminar, I could see the truth: i9 and Frank Fiume were two separate entities. *That* was the epiphany. As I wrote in my workbook: "I am *more* than you, and you are more than me." So while I was grateful beyond words for all that i9 had done for me, my life could no longer be defined by its success.

My hope was that the i9 brand would far outlive me, that it would have an impact on generations of kids, and make a positive change in their lives forever. But my self-worth had to be *separate* and apart from the business. That realization was life-changing.

LIFE IN THE FAST LANE

- When you are driving success 24/7, don't forget to take care of your body. Nothing substitutes for healthy food and exercise.
- Make sure you have a solid non-compete agreement. You never know who will try and steal your secrets.
- Make sure you know WHY you do WHAT you do. Someone may rip off your systems, but they can't appropriate your culture.
- Only your own decisions or lack thereof will determine your destiny when you are facing forces beyond your control.
- When the business becomes bigger than you, it may be time to hire a president and COO to take the operations burden off you.
- Move beyond just knowing *what* your values are. Prioritize them in a new sequence and take action on them.
- Formulate a vision that will take you through life's inevitable challenges, no matter what the pain.
- Reject the idea that you and your business are one and the same— they're not.
- The success of your business does not define your self-worth.

Chapter Nine

THE BIG TIME

After I came home from the Tony Robbins seminar, I never again reverted to being so overly obsessed with the business and equating financial success with fulfillment. Even though I had always been highly involved in my kids' lives and valued our family time, what changed was that I began to be emotionally present. My mind stopped continuously wandering back to i9 as it had done before.

At the office, I learned to appreciate even the little annoying things in life that had typically frustrated me in the past. For example, when times were stressful at the office, I realized that there was good in people, and I could view a problem from their vantage point. I could better empathize with their thinking and what they were going through. I became less defensive as I came to realize that nobody was out to hurt or take advantage of me.

When franchisees complained, I was able to see that it was nothing personal toward the company or me. It was nothing more than a cry for help. Once I understood this, I became more patient and understanding, and I was willing to coach them through whatever it was that was bothering them. I had never looked at franchisees that way before. Nor had I experienced gratitude for their business the way I did now. I felt like I was becoming the man I wanted to be—less reactive, more reflective, less thankless, and more appreciative.

Ironically, I would sorely need some of this newfound wisdom. While i9 had seemed immune to the effects of the Great Recession, by spring 2009, the momentum of our franchise sales was starting to slow down. We were receiving hundreds of inquiries from potential franchisees every month, many of them people who had been recently laid off from their companies. Here they were at our doorstep, with limited resources and no way of sustaining their lifestyle while the business got off the ground. As much as we wanted new business, we were very selective and turned many of them away. Fortunately for us, during this post-crash period, while many franchisors went under or resorted to selling overseas franchises, the royalties from our existing franchisees kept us afloat. We stayed focused on making our existing franchisees as profitable as possible.

"DON'T SOLVE A PROBLEM BY CREATING A DIFFERENT, BIGGER PROBLEM."

Because we sold only twenty-three franchises in 2009 (a 40 percent drop versus 2008), Brian and I agreed that we would accept some franchisees as part-time owners, allowing them to keep their day jobs while their i9 Sports business grew. It ended up being a terrible idea to award franchises to people who didn't have the money or the courage to quit their full-time jobs. Why? Because running a franchise properly required full-time effort.

We quickly discovered that part-timers were just not responsible. They were tuned out: Since they were not fully committed, they never spent enough time or money marketing their leagues, nor did they attend all of the training, educational webinars, and conferences mandated by us. Since they weren't generating enough revenue, they either continued to flounder or started exiting the system. The lesson in our experiment to subsidize part-time franchise owners? It came down to a mantra I'd always used, one that kept repeating itself now in my brain: Don't solve a problem by creating a different, bigger problem. And that's exactly what we had done. Yes, it was fixable, and over the next three years, we slowly closed down the part-time franchises and never offered that option again.

TIMING IS EVERYTHING

Though we haven't yet reached the one thousand franchise locations I had envisioned having in the U.S., I'm very grateful that we have been able to grow into the largest franchised sports league in the country, operating programs in over nine hundred community locations (some generating more than $1,000,000 in revenue) and we're still growing.

As I look back on the entire history of i9 now, I can see that timing is everything. Had we not had the courage to take a leap of faith in 2003 to found i9 Sports (or double-down and fix our broken business model in 2005), we never would've accumulated a sufficient number of franchisees to generate the royalties we needed to keep the lights on. This was especially crucial during the recession when our sale of new franchises precipitously decreased. Strangely, the Great Recession helped us because it staved off any potential national competition to i9 for another three years, far longer than I ever anticipated. This gave our franchisees the chance to maximize their advantage and expand quickly.

UNDERSTAND YOUR AUDIENCE

In June 2009, after a family trip out West, it was time for i9's national meeting in Denver. Unlike prior meeting speeches, when my presentation focused on unveiling our latest product or major software update, I wanted this speech to go beyond the predictable. I knew that competition from other companies was inevitable, so I needed our franchisees to open up their minds and think strategically about expansion and quality control.

My speech's theme was "Blue Ocean Strategy," inspired by the book of the same name. (The book's subtitle is *How to Create Uncontested Market Space and Make the Competition Irrelevant*.) The author, W. Chan Kim, argues that leading companies succeed not by battling competitors, but by systematically creating "blue oceans" of uncontested market space ripe for growth. The strategy represents the simultaneous pursuit of high product differentiation and low cost, thereby making competition irrelevant. Having recently finished the book, I was excited to give the franchise owners a peek into my world of business strategies, and I anticipated that they would eat it up. Boy, was I wrong!

It flopped, big time. I may have implemented countless strategies inspired by the dozens of business books I'd read, but that fact was irrelevant here. In the faces of a group of about one hundred franchisees facing me, I saw total apathy. The more I explained my theme, the more puzzled they looked. Although I was pretty embarrassed by the cold reception, I did learn a valuable lesson that day: You need to understand your audience and appreciate *their* point of view and greatest need. Franchise owners didn't want to hear strategic generalities about where i9 was headed.

Instead, they wanted to know specifically what I was going to do to help improve their business—and when, as I'd always done in the past. I'd let them down by not delivering something new, and I left Colorado determined to come back and give the keynote speech of my life at our next conference.

LIVE ON AIR, DECEMBER 30, 2009

"Look straight ahead into the camera," said the unfamiliar voice coming out of my earpiece. "And at all times, wait until the host is finished talking before you respond."

"Got it!" I answered.

This was i9's big break. The PR firm we'd hired had booked a TV interview for me on *Fox Business News*, a live broadcast from New York. A national media appearance like this, the dream of any entrepreneur, had been years in the making, and I wanted it to be perfect. I knew going in that I'd only have a few minutes to promote i9 Sports. I decided that no matter what the host, Eric Bolling, asked me, I was going to spew out bullet points I'd memorized about our company. This was my five minutes to tell the world exactly what I wanted them to hear.

Even if I was asked, "Why is the sky blue?" I was ready to respond, "i9 Sports is about teaching kids how to win with grace and lose with dignity!"

At the start, as the red light of the camera went on, Bolling asked me what made i9 Sports different from other youth leagues. And I jumped right in, hitting all the hot buttons for parents: "We're about fun, safety, and convenience; we practice on the same day as the games; there are no fundraisers, no tryouts, no drafts, and no parental politics." Bam. I was really pleased with how I performed under the pressure of the interview and quickly regrouped with Nadine and the kids, who had proudly watched it live in the next room of the studio.

What a high! While the national news was mostly all doom and gloom about the economy and terrorism, i9's media coverage was a bright spot with a positive message that was ever expanding. We had newspaper articles in *The Wall Street Journal*, *USA Today*, *The Tampa Tribune*, and others—and television interviews on HBO's

"OUR COMPANY PROFILE WAS GOLDEN."

Real Sports as well as on the local NBC-affiliate morning news show. Our company profile was golden.

EXPANSION

You get rewarded in public for what you've intensely practiced in private, and that thought perfectly described what was happening at i9. Despite a free fall of new franchise sales in 2010, with only a dismal seven franchises sold (down from twenty-three in 2009 and thirty-eight in 2008), the foundation of our business remained strong. That's because our existing franchisees were raking in $14 million in revenue nationwide. I remained steadfast and refused to give in to negative news media talk about the Great Recession. I focused on how great companies such as Disney, Microsoft, and Apple had not only started during bad economic times but had thrived *during* the downturns. What we all had in common was that we didn't hunker down or operate defensively, waiting for the economy to magically recover. We weren't going to hide out under a rock until the media said the recession was over. Brian and I were hell-bent on operating in the same way we always had and regularly communicated that to our employees and franchise owners.

True, we couldn't sell a *new* franchise to save our lives. But every business has to create a united front. Brian and I agreed that this was no time to demonstrate fear or pull back in our attempts to proactively grow i9 long-term.

To this end, we repurchased the first franchise I'd sold in 2003, giving us a company-owned location to test new products and services in our own backyard in Tampa. We opened a customer service center in-house, freeing up our franchisees while delivering a consistent experience; and Brian brilliantly created a cash-flow planner that conveniently allowed franchisees to project future income based on their investment in marketing and additional staffing—and offering additional sports in expanded locations. That planner wasn't just an administrative tool, but rather a symbol of i9's belief in the future. This, along with establishing financial benchmarks, a focus on customer satisfaction scores, and a network scorecard, allowed franchisees to see how they ranked amongst their peers and did wonders for morale.

By 2012, it was time to find a new home for i9 Sports—a 12,400-square-foot rental office space located in a large industrial park in Riverview, centrally located for our employees. All thirty of our staff would finally be together under one roof. To me, the move to our new headquarters that November was a symbol of our tenacity during the Great Recession.

With my energy for i9 and Brian's steady leadership, our franchise revenues climbed to $19 million nationwide. I was grateful to have an effective team to delegate to and a support system that was designed to take some of the stress away from me.

WHAT GOES UP

But having a larger team and a bigger office did not stop me from continuing to take phendimetrazine. Beginning in 2011, I had noticed that the diet pills I'd been taking for years gradually lost their effectiveness. No longer was the medication helping me with weight loss, nor was the euphoric effect from it as reliable as it had been. I'd try to wean myself off the pills, knowing I needed to kick this thing for good. But then the withdrawal symptoms began: I'd begin feeling blue, and my appetite would come roaring back!

> **"DESPITE MY ATTEMPTS TO DECOMPRESS, MY BRAIN WAS FRIED."**

Within weeks, I'd see a spike in my weight, so I'd go back on the medication to control my weight and get the euphoria I needed—even though I'd later crash and feel incredibly fatigued. It was a vicious cycle. I believed that taking time off away from the business more and more would help remedy this. In the short run, when we did get away on vacations, it worked! Because I wasn't under stress and enjoyed every minute of the trips, I felt temporarily rejuvenated. However, the more trips we went on, the less I wanted to go back to i9. Despite my attempts to decompress, my brain was fried.

As I look back on it now, I was burned out—extra-crispy burnt. Feeling overwhelmed had turned into a state of despair. It seemed that my luck had run out. I felt like that copywriter in the Bradley Cooper movie *Limitless* who discovers an experimental drug that gives him superhuman abilities, though his entire life ultimately crashes and burns. In fact, when I saw *Limitless* in 2011, I remember saying, "Holy crap, that's *me*." Just like the character in the movie, I was on fire and about to burn down. And I knew why—but I kept plowing ahead, forcing myself to work hard at the office.

I bought a book by Dr. Alan Shelton called *Transforming Burnout—A Simple Guide to Self-Renewal*. In it, he argued that burnout is the result of a life *imbalance*—more specifically, a lack of commitment to one's spiritual needs. I couldn't disagree. It wasn't long after this that I had a nightmare about my dying. When I woke up the next morning, for the first time ever, I actually felt my mortality, an inevitability that had never been real to me in the past.

Was that normal for a forty-two-year-old? I guess you could say it was partially due to a midlife crisis. But despite this challenge, I remained grateful for all that was *good* in our lives—family time, business growth, and our income.

I continued to sweep the diet pill addiction under the carpet.

THE BIG TIME

- Take time to be emotionally present with those you love and empathize with those you work with.
- If a colleague complains or is angry, it is usually a cry for help. Be willing to coach them through whatever it is.
- Don't solve a problem by creating a different, bigger problem.
- Understand your audience (your employees or franchisees) and appreciate *their* point of view and greatest need.
- Get an effective team and a support system to take some of the stress away from you; be grateful for both of them.
- If you start to feel exhausted, find a way to get your life back in balance before you burn out.

Chapter Ten

WHAT REALLY MATTERS

M eanwhile, no matter how I felt mentally, the show had to go on
when it came to presiding over i9's 2011 national meeting, held
that July in Tampa. To make up for what had happened two years earlier during my last keynote speech—the "Blue Ocean" flop, as I like to
call it—I had to redeem myself. For over a year, I'd been working closely
with my team to develop what I believed would give franchisees a slew
of big surprises, ones that would blow their minds.

I took to the stage and announced "The Big 5" initiatives:

- i9 Sports tee-ball for kids ages three to six

- Competitive/travel flag football program called "i9 Elite"

- A mobile website in anticipation of the explosion of
  mobile devices

- "Season Pass," which would allow a child to play as much as
  they wanted to for one low monthly fee, giving franchisees
  ongoing residual revenue

- An option for franchisees to create a nonprofit organization,
  giving disadvantaged kids the opportunity to play in i9 Sports

As I unveiled each of these innovations, the audience of 130 franchisees and employees all cheered loudly! Now I was speaking their language. It was an out-of-the-park home run, the rollout flawless, truly the pinnacle of my career at i9.

Especially after what had happened in Denver, the reaction I got felt like total redemption. I left that conference on a high, feeling that this had been the best national meeting we ever had. Most everyone else agreed.

But I soon learned that I had missed a very important lesson—a shift was occurring throughout the organization that I failed to anticipate. There was a small contingent of franchisees who spoke up, saying that they wanted more collaborative input in the rollout of new products and services and the overall direction of the company—and fewer of my surprises. The organization had grown well beyond top-down leadership, and the idea of a collaborative think tank for all initiatives moving forward was difficult for me to embrace as the founder.

During this period, I thought back to the epiphany I'd had at the Tony Robbins seminar—mainly that i9 and Frank Fiume were *not* one and the same. Clearly the organization was evolving for the better, yet I began to question where I fit in and whether I might be suffering from *founderitis*.[4]

---

4 Founder's syndrome (also known as *founderitis*) is a popular term for a difficulty faced by organizations when one or more founders maintain disproportionate power and influence following the effective initial establishment of the project, leading to a wide range of problems for the organization.

ONE SHOT IN LIFE

I've read that one of the most common things people say at the end of their lives is: "I wish I hadn't worked so hard!" All too late, they realize that they didn't spend enough time with the people they loved most—their friends and family. Instead, they were often consumed with work, trapped on the treadmill of a daily routine. I didn't want that to happen to me.

"MY ATTITUDE WAS THAT YOU ONLY GET ONE SHOT IN LIFE."

With Brian essentially running the company (as he had now done for four years), I no longer went into the office every day, and I felt freer than ever to take the time I needed with Nadine and the kids. I found myself leaving more and more of the day-to-day operations to Brian, who said:

> I interpreted Frank's ability to leave the office as trust. He was always fully engaged and in tune with the business whether he was physically there or not. He'd log into our software, study the detailed franchisee notes, and review the business metrics, then conference with me about anything essential. But on a day-to-day basis, I was able to take the weight off him, so he could go off on a vacation and take advantage of the time when his kids were young.

My attitude was that you only get one shot in life, and as a family we were going to take it. After all, ours was a unique situation: Our kids were being homeschooled, I didn't have to be in the office every day, and we were more financially secure than ever. So, beginning in 2009, the next seven years were filled with family adventures, many of them on a Disney cruise. In fact, we crammed in twenty-four family cruises during that time period—not to mention the fourteen prior to that, bringing our total number of ocean getaways to thirty-eight!

Our adventures took us to fascinating locations, not only in the Caribbean and Mexico, but also throughout Europe. Back home, I fulfilled my longtime dream of visiting all thirty Major League Baseball stadiums. In fact, we managed to visit not only all thirty stadiums on our then-current list, we also pushed our record to thirty-three since a few teams we'd already visited opened new ballparks.

Was all the time and effort invested in the family trips worth it? Absolutely. Having money is meaningless if you don't use it to create a fulfilling lifestyle. And we squeezed in more crazy adventures with the kids in a fifteen-year period than most people do in a lifetime, visiting twenty-six U.S. states and over a dozen foreign countries.

REMEMBERING YOUR PURPOSE

Back at the office, we had gotten so caught up in the business of i9—marketing strategies for registering kids, technology updates, merchandise vendor contracts, financial management and human resources, franchisee and employee morale—that we sometimes forgot that we were in the business of changing lives! I was reminded of i9's true mission and meaning one night when one of our i9 franchisees brought to my attention a TV news report about a Florida family who had lost their house in a fire.

One of the kids in the family was featured on-camera, wearing an i9 Sports jersey, extremely upset that everything in the house was gone, all of it destroyed in the blaze. The local franchisee figured out who the customer was and called up the mom. "I'm so sorry to hear about your home. Is there anything we can do to help?"

"We don't even know where to begin," she told him tearfully. "We've lost everything. I can't believe you were thoughtful enough to reach out to me. Actually, my son's sportsmanship medal had burned with the house, and that was the one thing he really wanted more than anything else. He was so proud of his i9 medal and is heartbroken over losing it."

I went home that night, and as the four us sat down for dinner, I began telling the story of the fire to Nadine and the kids. I barely got the words out of my mouth before I got all choked up. I don't think the kids had ever seen me break down before. But the gratitude I felt, combined with the rush of being able to contribute, had overloaded my emotions—in a good way.

We sent the boy a new medal right away, and it was at that moment that I realized that i9 had a more profound impact on kids than I had ever imagined. That medal may have only cost a few dollars to us, but it was priceless to the boy. To me, there was something amazing about a young child feeling such enormous pride in an award given for exemplary behavior. It wasn't a participation medal for doing nothing, but a unique award for being the best team player, for helping others, which was that particular week's sportsmanship value.

It wasn't long after that experience that a mom in Ohio posted this on our Facebook page:

The night before his recent game, my five-year-old told me that he was going to dream about scoring his first touchdown and winning a sportsmanship medal. Game day: HE SCORES HIS FIRST TOUCHDOWN and wins the medal! The look of determination as he ran down the field for a touchdown—his expression of pride as he heard the cheers for him—was unforgettable!

As I read the post, once again I thought, *That's why i9 Sports is in business.* When I first founded the company, never in my wildest dreams did I envision that we'd be creating moments that would be remembered forever. Events like these were a strong reminder that I was fulfilling my purpose in life, a goal that had consumed me since childhood. All in all, my renewed passion for i9 came just at the right time.

WE'RE BEING SUED?

"You haven't truly experienced franchising until your first franchisee lawsuit!" Those were the wise words of my long-time franchise attorney after learning that one of our Florida franchisees had been cheating us out of royalties and merchandise revenue for years, while operating a separate youth sports business under another name. He had also purchased non-branded products from an unapproved vendor and operated a tackle football league and mixed martial arts program while cross-marketing it to our i9 customer base. We stood our ground, pursued the case, and won—but at great cost, especially in time and energy.

Shortly after that, a brazen franchisee in Colorado illegally sold part of his territory to a previously rejected candidate, an employee of his. He even went so far as to attempt to buy an additional territory that he planned to immediately flip, though he never told the employee about the swindle. Sadly, the employee thought he was a full-fledged i9 franchise owner and intended to come down to one of our training classes. When he found out he had no rights whatsoever, he wound up suing *us* for his down payment to the crooked franchisee. And after the whole mess was straightened out, we won, but once again, the action cost us thousands in legal fees.

Clearly we had entered a new era in i9 Sports—with all innocence lost. More than ever, I began to recognize that to be successful in franchising, you needed to be Steve Jobs, a politician, and a policeman all rolled into one. While I loved the showmanship part of the job—unveiling new products and services—and I relished the impact we were making on thousands of kids each year—I definitely hated the politics and intrigue. It was exhausting, and I didn't want to lose my sense of passion when it came to i9.

WHAT REALLY MATTERS

- As your business grows, embrace more collaboration, not top-down leadership.
- Vow not to be the person who realizes too late they have forgotten to spend enough time with their friends and family.
- Get away and relax! You will remember those times forever.
- Remind yourself of your purpose. In the case of i9, we were in the business of changing lives!
- In every business where you understand your purpose, you are potentially creating moments for customers to remember forever.

Chapter Eleven

UNDER SIEGE

With some much-needed space between me and i9, I began to focus my attention on home life, especially on the idea of building a big new house with more land. I soon stumbled upon a 4.25-acre piece of land with a huge pond on Miller Road in nearby Valrico. The house was custom-designed from scratch, with me involved every step of the way. After countless revisions of the architectural plans, the house ballooned to 6,300 square feet—including five bedrooms, six bathrooms, and a six-car garage, plus an exercise room, a theater, an office, an outdoor kitchen, and a 50,000-gallon resort-size swimming pool.

I realize now that my preoccupation with the new house was partly an escape from i9 and partly to satisfy my appetite for bigger and better. Impressive as it turned out to be, it wasn't long before I realized it was overkill. I was embarrassed by the enormity of this house. Buying stuff didn't make me happy.

First of all, possessions are *temporary* by nature. The novelty of anything new always begins to *fade*. That initial rush of excitement never lasts. Second, there is always something new right around the corner, so everything you buy has obsolescence built into it. Third, all this stuff takes maintenance and can lead to obligation and burden. The search for happiness in possessions is always short-lived because shopping doesn't quench our desire for contentment.

Progress leads to happiness, as Tony Robbins would say. I was trying to fulfill my need for happiness through the stages of building the house over the course of a year. Not surprisingly, once the progress ended and the house was built, I was unfulfilled again.

Happiness can be found by doing fulfilling work with a *purpose*. It's being productive and making a difference. It's being grateful and kind. Most importantly, it's having deep connections to the people we love, sharing with them *life-changing experiences* that become more meaningful than any material object ever could be.

Experiences such as a family trip or a personal development seminar allow you to learn a lot about yourself—and about what you *really* want in life. Looking back, I see that building "Miller" was my attempt to find happiness in materialistic terms, because I was no longer fulfilled in my work.

I had devoted a decade of my life to the success of my company. The measure of this success was that I was not needed in the same way I had been for so long.

It was around this time that a quote from Steve Jobs hit me:

> *I have looked in the mirror every morning and asked myself: "If today were the last day of my life, would I want to do what I am about to do today?" And whenever the answer has been "No" for too many days in a row, I know I need to change something.*

That's exactly how I felt. My newfound freedom from the company's demands on me didn't feel as great as I thought it would.

Something had to change.

This feeling meshed with the epiphany I had had at Date with Destiny—that the company and myself were two different entities.

But if I wasn't the company, then who *was* I? An identity crisis was brewing. My feeling that something was missing at i9 certainly wasn't affecting its record-breaking success. In 2013, our franchisees revenue had soared to $24 million (up from $19 million in 2012). Good as these numbers were, getting new franchisees was hit or miss. Even when we procured a new franchisee, our $35,000-fee was immediately swallowed up by marketing budgets, salaries, and commissions.

How could we take *control* over the rate of opening new locations?

Our CPA, Brian, Kim, and I brainstormed about how to turn around five years of stalled growth regarding franchise sales. Maybe the answer was taking massive action by opening *company-owned* locations. (Warning sign: Don't solve a problem by creating a bigger one!) In addition to selling franchises, we would now *become* the franchisee, using our proven system to strategically open i9 franchises in available markets of the country. We would be playing both sides of the fence like some franchisors do. Our marketing efforts in adjacent territories would benefit existing franchisees. It was a win-win for everyone. And we would also contribute 1 percent of our revenue to the national brand fund for advertising purposes, just as other franchisees had to.

FULL THROTTLE

Weeks of behind-closed-doors meetings followed. Kim, Brian, and I calculated the start-up cost (about $500,000), the break-even ratio analysis, and a long-range growth forecast. Brian's brilliant name for the new strategy was "Full Throttle," and we kept all details of it confidential for six months until our 2013 national meeting in San Antonio. In the months leading up to it, the hours were long, but I loved it. I was reinvigorated. My company needed me again in a way that put me back in my element—a project I could run with along with my team without needing buy-in from others. The final plan was to inaugurate the launch with four company-owned locations in the spring of 2014, along with a new consumer website, targeted toward our main customer: moms. The goal was presenting a format that made it easier for parents to register for a league in geographical locations that were most convenient to them.

When I arrived in San Antonio with Nadine and the kids, I was irritable and difficult to please because I wanted everything to go perfectly. My mood didn't improve when I walked into our meeting space at the San Antonio Hilton Hotel. We were crammed into a small room with little aisle space, there was no room in the back for refreshments, and the stage lighting was terrible. The event coordinators quickly huddled together with the hotel staff and began to rectify the mess, but we had definitely started off on the wrong foot.

The meeting kicked off with the welcome reception, and our franchisees seemed in great spirits as they poured into the conference room. They hadn't seen each other in two years, and they were excited to mingle with their peers while hoping to gain new insights into growing their businesses. Behind the scenes, I continued to wonder how they would react to my Full Throttle presentation. Would they be receptive to it, as excited about it as Brian, Kim, and I were? Or would they somehow view it as a threat?

My presentation began with an update on our flat franchise sales, which had had a negative impact on our national ad fund budget that prevented us from larger scale advertising of the brand. The lack of new franchise volume, I explained, prevented everyone from getting lower prices on jerseys and equipment. I seemed to have the entire room with me when I launched into the solution to the problem.

I began:

Introducing Full Throttle: A growth strategy that parallels and complements our franchise sales model by aggressively opening company-owned locations while continuing to sell franchises nationwide

If the "Blue Ocean" flop was bad, this one was even worse! By the time I was finished with my fifteen-minute summary of Full Throttle, you could hear a pin drop in that room. Evidently the franchisees had misinterpreted what I had said, concluding that i9 was exiting franchising—a thought that scared them to death. They couldn't figure out what our proposal would mean for their business.

While I tried my best to put their minds at ease, explaining that Full Throttle was a "parallel strategy," not a threat to their business, the mood in the room remained tense. Fear and uncertainty reigned supreme. Brian and I had many times discussed how the franchisees might react to the news, but we had clearly underestimated how the reaction would be. As Brian said:

> In the end, franchisees viewed our initiative as a threat, a sign that we were going to abandon the franchise model, which they took great offense to. And even though we reassured them, a lot of fear was involved. And in retrospect, we could have done a better job in allaying those fears when we rolled it out.

No matter what the franchisee resistance was, my role was to gain their acceptance, whether they liked it or not. Kim said:

> Frank can't stand to be confined and doesn't like to have to answer to anybody. When the business got really big, he hated when he had to play the game to make franchisees happy in order to get them to buy into his ideas. He knew what was right for i9 and wanted to run with it.

What's the big lesson in all this? Although we chose to unveil Full Throttle as a surprise, I should have gotten the franchisees involved early in the thought process by sharing our rationale and forming a committee that could have provided valuable feedback as we developed the initiative along the way. Instead, I rammed it down their throats with a fancy PowerPoint presentation on stage at a huge national meeting. Ouch.

As Brian has often said, if you don't communicate well, people will fill in the blanks—oftentimes with fear. And as I shared with my kids who witnessed the debacle firsthand, "To be a leader, you've got to be thick-skinned. Criticism comes with the territory. You've got to expect it. The franchisees reacted the way they did because they were scared about losing their business, and I should have communicated better."

> ## "IF YOU DON'T COMMUNICATE WELL, PEOPLE WILL FILL IN THE BLANKS— OFTENTIMES WITH FEAR."

The next day, with much fanfare I unveiled a new consumer mobile website that we had been working on for nearly a year. It was a huge hit with its clean design and the animated photos of smiling i9 kids intended to reduce the time it took for parents to register their kids online. The result: A whopping 154 percent revenue growth with registrations soaring from $15.7 million (2011) to $40 million (2017). The 2013 national meeting concluded with mixed reviews, with most franchisees excited about the new website but uncomfortable with Full Throttle.

STALKERS, SCAMMERS, AND SHOCK JOCKS

With the national meeting behind us, it was full steam ahead with Full Throttle, or so I thought. Less than two weeks after the national meeting, I received a frantic call from one of our franchisees in Florida. "Frank, I'm so sorry to bother you, but I need you to know that there's a guy who I considered bringing on as an investor in my franchise— but no longer. He's been sending me a flurry of texts tonight making physical threats against you and the company because his application to become an i9 franchisee was rejected."

"Huh? Who? Hell, I'm not even involved with approving candidates anymore," I told him. "Let me look into this. I'll get back to you tomorrow."

Before I could even call him back to explain, he called me again. "Frank, I think we may need to get an order of protection. This guy is still making crazy threats against you."

A few weeks later I found myself in a courtroom, where the judge issued an order of protection against the stalker, who was now prohibited from making any contact with us or anyone related to i9 Sports.

Not long after that, we got hit with another aberration—the discovery that one of our newest franchisees had a previous conviction for running a Ponzi scheme. He had bilked sixty-three investors out of $44 million, after which he spent five years in jail. Distressingly, this franchisee had slipped through the cracks of our background check process due to some faulty state reporting. It would take months, and would cost us thousands in legal fees, before we succeeded in legally removing this bad apple from i9.

With this fire put out, yet another one popped up in its place.

One night on my drive home, I was listening to Sports Radio, only half paying attention, when I was shocked to hear:

Hey, have you guys heard about this local company called i9 Sports? What a joke. I was on their website. Listen to this. They say they're all about fun, safety, and convenience—teaching good sportsmanship, and then I find a link to, are you ready, a franchise opportunity. What is this world coming to? Where are the days when volunteer dads would run Little League for free because they wanted to play ball with their kids? Now, it's all about profit. We've got this guy Fiume selling franchises for $35,000! For what? i9 Sports has privatized and commercialized the all-American pastime of youth sports. Disgusting.

I was livid that i9 was being portrayed as a company of ambitious hypocrites, attempting to put nonprofits like Little League out of business. I knew that all this criticism and negativity was *not* a reflection of the truth or our company's values.

Ruthless unfair behavior like this taught me a few important lessons about dealing with criticism.

I wrote the following to my staff in a memo:

- ***Don't Take It Personally**—Whether it's a competitor, a dissatisfied parent, or a local sportswriter who slams you—you are not the one they hate. You must be emotionally detached from such critiques. When it comes to the critics, they just don't believe what you believe in, period. Just know you will never make them happy. And if you do struggle with taking negative comments personally, I highly recommend two great books by Don Miguel Ruiz—*The Four Agreements *and*The Fifth Agreement.

- ***Take No Action**—Remember, news cycles don't last long, and bad press fades quickly. Not responding to negative PR limits the attention given to it, whereas reacting angrily quickly validates the reporter's claims, only shining a harsher light on the issue.*

- ***When to Contact a News Reporter (Print Journalist)**—Do so only to correct a factual error, but leave out all emotion, and never argue. No reporter wants to be proven wrong. You will only fuel the flames.*

- ***When to Issue a Public Response**—Sometimes in a crisis, bad press can damage a business's reputation. If so, a straightforward news release offers the most efficient means of delivering information.*

Little did Mr. Radio Shock-Jock remember that his station had had no problem taking my advertising money for commercials that aired on his show back when we were getting started in 2003! Nor did he know that i9 had a few thousand local raving fans, including influential radio personalities from his very station, school board members, police and fire commissioners, celebrities, and current and former professional athletes in all four major sports, including several head coaches in the NFL!

As I thought about the sequence of recent events—the far-from-ideal national meeting, the stalker, the Ponzi scheme franchisee, the shock jock radio personality—it occurred to me that in the grand scheme of things, these were all little nuisances that happen when you're the largest youth sports franchise organization in the United States. This was nothing compared to the pain I had endured when the company was on death's doorstep nearly a decade earlier.

The real-life question is: *How* do you handle a crisis?

First, you need to know that every successful business brings with it an ever-greater possibility of crisis—and threats from every direction. Of course, there will be people criticizing you, misbehaving, even betraying you, causing you a multitude of headaches! But that's to be expected. That's business. Deal with it and move on.

As Martin Luther King Jr. once said: "Your measure as a leader is not where you stand in moments of comfort and convenience, but where you stand in times of challenge and controversy."

If we hadn't been successful, nobody would've talked about us in the first place. As 2013 came to a close, our 10th anniversary was our most successful year—and the least boring, for sure!

WHEN YOU ARE UNDER SIEGE

- Look out for the warning signs that you are heading for burnout.
- Beware of the race for bigger and better in your personal life. The search for happiness in possessions is always short-lived because buying things doesn't quench our desire for contentment.
- Happiness comes from doing fulfilling work with a *purpose*.
- Before you roll out a new policy, make sure you consider the fears it could produce in your teams.
- Every successful business brings the possibility of threats from every direction.

PART FOUR

Chapter Twelve

WHEN THE TOP OF THE MOUNTAIN IS NOT ENOUGH

By early 2014, Project Full Throttle's initiative to open company-owned locations was fully underway. Brian and I even focused on a ten-year expansion plan to build out the rest of the United States with i9 Sports locations. Not to plan for the future is where too many businesses go wrong. As I had learned, there are always two businesses you've got to manage—the one you're in and the one you're becoming.

After much analysis, I recommended to Brian that we start our national build-out by focusing on four territories for company-owned franchises: North Seattle (Washington), Boise (Idaho), McKinney (Texas), and Memphis (Tennessee). Each offered outstanding demographics, similar to those of our best-performing territories. The national expansion was an all-out effort of staff, time, and money, driven by my core philosophy: "We either do it right or not at all."

"WE EITHER DO IT RIGHT OR NOT AT ALL."

Utilizing a healthy marketing budget, we got outstanding results: The four locations acquired over 4,000 members, of which 1,750 became paid registrations, making the total haul of the spring season $214,000. The franchisees soon realized there was nothing to fear. In fact, our impressive results created intrigue and allowed us to share out in detail how we did it at a free one-and-a-half-day training at our office.

With the success of the first four company-owned locations behind us, Brian and I kept running with our heads down, opening an additional *eight* locations later that fall. We were putting in enormous hours, determined to make the business grow via company-owned locations *and* new franchise sales, but the more locations we opened, the more the complexity of the business multiplied exponentially.

Over the next two years, we opened sixteen locations, but the bigger we got (with a staff of well over one hundred), the more our expansion went off the rails. In fact, our company-owned location financials were now hemorrhaging, exceeding a loss of over $500,000 in 2014. While we had expected to lose about that much in start-up costs, our projection to break even was at least three, probably four years away.

More importantly, it occurred to me that we were built on being a great franchisor and supporting franchisees; we were not a company-owned organization structured to manage remote employees.

The challenge I didn't anticipate was that by splitting i9 in two—half franchisor and half company-owned—it was beginning to tear our company culture apart, with our own in-house employees wondering which side of the house was going to succeed long-term and were they on the winning side?

We eventually closed or sold all of our company-owned locations, with the exception of our backyard, the East Tampa Bay franchise (that we repurchased back in 2009), which continues to be among the most successful of any i9 Sports franchise nationwide.

IT'S NOT YOU. IT'S ME.

I had forgotten to follow my own strict rule: Never solve a problem by creating a new, bigger one.

If I had to do it all over again, I would have expanded much more slowly. The company-owned location strategy could've worked if we had simply slowed down and worked out the bugs first. Speed kills. We didn't have our remote employee recruitment and management issues resolved, yet we plowed ahead, opening new locations at a rapid pace in an attempt to offset the fixed employee costs we had as infrastructure.

I give Brian, Kim, and the team a ton of credit for their unwavering dedication to try and make this work. They gave it their all and then some. Brian was willing to stick it out and see it through, but I talked him into pulling the plug. Kim was reluctantly relieved that we would end the company-owned location initiative.

The two-year saga of i9's company-owned expansion was exhausting and my biggest disappointment. While our customers were happy, and our franchisees were satisfied, I was personally unfulfilled to the point of no return. Where would I go from here?

The needs of the business no longer matched the blueprint of what I enjoyed most. The entrepreneurial creativity and innovation were now driven by office meetings, advisory councils, and task force approvals from others. It was just a by-product of how the business had evolved. It and I had simply grown apart.

Yes, we could be very proud and impressed with i9's financials, which continued to soar: By the end of 2014, franchise revenues had hit $30 million. However, for me, it was never only about making money. I wanted to make a difference.

At this point in our office culture, unfortunately, as happens in many quickly expanding companies, cracks in the armor of our office team were beginning to show. Our largest department, the Customer Service Center, was comprised of twenty to twenty-eight part-time reps fielding phone calls nationwide. As Kim recalls, "Suddenly we doubled in size and had twenty new people in the office—part-timers and seasonal workers who had no true investment in our company and felt no real connection to it. So, rather than feeling like a close-knit family, we were suddenly bumping into strangers in the coffee room, a crazy dynamic that made Frank so uncomfortable."

Overall, we now had 115 employees split between the Florida headquarters and our field staff. As we had become a so-called large employer, even firing somebody became a big production. We had to bring our human resources rep into the loop before giving someone the ax. I began to think about what Tony Robbins would say about all this. I remembered him talking about the importance of appreciating life even when things aren't going your way, because the reality is that the more people you have working for you, the more likely somebody is going to screw things up!

> ## "I BEGAN TO THINK THAT MAYBE I WASN'T THE RIGHT PERSON TO LEAD SUCH A LARGE ORGANIZATION."

I began to think that maybe I wasn't the right person to lead such a large organization. Yet the guilt of leaving i9 behind led me right back to it. After all, this was my mission in life, wasn't it? This was my purpose. Yes, i9 and Frank Fiume were two separate entities, but if this was my mission in life, how could I possibly leave it?

THE ONE WHO IGNITES THE SPARK

Nadine once observed:

> *I'd see how much the staff appreciated Frank and benefited from his presence. Just him walking into his office was enough for them*

to become more energized because of the energy that he brought with him. Though he didn't want to be as fully involved in the administrative side of running i9, I told him to just go into your office and do whatever you want to do on your computer, but BE THERE IN BODY. And while he eventually didn't want to be there at all, I was concerned about how Brian and Kim were going to feel.

Don't get me wrong: I was enormously grateful for the lifestyle that the company afforded me. And I still wanted to be productive in the business, but I began questioning in my own head, *How much longer can I do this?* While I was still capable of functioning at the office and taking control when needed, I now felt like a fish out of water, uncomfortable in the very company that I created.

I came to the conclusion that I was *not* the right person to lead a big company like i9 into the future. Whereas Brian was more temperamentally suited to the role of CEO, expert at overseeing employees and masterminding the administrative side of things, I was more of a start-up guy—the one who ignites the spark and turns a vision into reality.

TOP OF THE GAME. EMPTY INSIDE.

In any case, because of my *emotional* state, I was withdrawing more and more. At first, I started coming into the office only two or three times a week, and later I cut back to just once a week. During all the stress of the tumultuous events from 2013 to 2014, I had stopped taking diet pills through sheer force of will. But by September 2014, my weight had gone from 175 to 193 pounds. Because I was desperate to peel off twenty pounds before I hit 200, I restarted the phendimetrazine, combining it with a pre-workout drink loaded with caffeine followed by a super-intense workout. I suddenly had enormous energy, focus, and endurance—more than I'd ever experienced before. In fact, within six months, my weight plummeted from 193 to 163, and I could wear the same size jeans as my fourteen-year-old son. For all appearances, I looked fit, but it remained to be seen if the energy level I induced artificially was going to be a risk worth taking.

During the last half of 2014, I struggled more and more with the disconnect between i9's booming success and my persistent feelings of deep discontentment. The last eighteen months had been turbulent. We overcame the mutiny at the national meeting in San Antonio; the stalkers and scammers; and the unjust publicity. On top of that, we threw ourselves "full throttle" into opening company-owned locations.

The result was that despite the overall booming financial health of i9, I still felt unfulfilled—having success but not enjoying it, despite i9's meteoric rise.

No one could dispute our track record: After eleven years of running with my head down, i9 had over 200,000 kids playing across thirty-three states—with our network-wide revenue eclipsing $30 million annually (and growing 15 to 20 percent per year). We were clearly at the top of our game, yet I felt totally empty inside. How could that be? It was clear: My vision for i9 was now complete, and I had no new dream to replace it.

"I HAD NO NEW DREAM TO REPLACE IT."

Even with the big numbers and all the accolades, I struggled with my desire to lead the company. I felt dead-ended and guilty, imprisoned by the belief that i9 Sports seemed to be my only purpose in life. I thought my mission was over. I know most people won't understand what I'm saying because they think the end goal of starting a business is to be "successful." But what does that even mean? Once you reach the goal of success, you *then* can be happy, able to relax and enjoy the fruits of your labor—right? What happens when you finally get to the top of the mountain, and you experience a big letdown? Then what? That's exactly where I was.

The truth was, I had never been motivated by money for money's sake. Don't get me wrong: I wanted to be wealthy. However, my focus was always on winning, on beating the competition to a pulp, on making i9 Sports as successful as it could possibly be. I didn't put my personal desire for money ahead of reinvesting it back into the company to make it grow. The more people we impacted (the kids, the parents, the volunteer coaches, the employees, the franchisees), the more money we made. What was passing me by was the fact that the measure of wealth you achieve is in proportion to the impact you make on others' lives—the value you provide to someone else.

But now I was just going through the motions, feeling like a prisoner in my own company. I felt desperate and stuck because all of our financial eggs were in the i9 Sports basket. I felt obligated to stay, even though I was mentally checked out. Just the sight of my dedicated employees working so hard made me feel even guiltier about my negative thoughts. It was an excruciating conflict—to like my employees and be liked so much by them, yet to be unhappy at the same time.

SIX HUMAN NEEDS

I linked my state of mind to a lack of fulfillment based upon the six human needs Tony Robbins talks about—certainty, variety, significance, love and connection, growth, and contribution. I wasn't feeling much *certainty* because I was no longer driving creativity and innovation as the needs of the business evolved. While you could say there was *variety* at the office, having a stalker or a PR crisis wasn't exactly the kind of *uncertainty or variety* I was looking for. Nor was I feeling needed any longer. Hence, my need for *significance* and *growth* had flatlined.

The only thing that really kept me going was the *love and connection* I felt from my employees. I had so many happy memories with my staff as we enjoyed laughs while dining at restaurants away from Tampa on trips around the country to visit franchisees. Back at home, whether it was taking them all on a fun-filled overnight retreat to Disney World or bonding with them each week on our company softball team, the camaraderie ran deep, and it was an asset that enhanced all of our lives. I even took a few of the courageous ones to a Tony Robbins event, part of my belief in the indispensable value of personal development.

And of course, I also felt a deep sense of *contribution*, having impacted millions of kids' lives with a sports program that left them with a lifetime of memories. I valued the satisfaction of knowing I had helped many franchisees achieve financial independence. I was always touched when they came up to me, thanking me for having the courage to start i9 and sharing their gratitude for welcoming them to be a part of it. That was my legacy.

But in the end, while I loved i9 with all my heart, I no longer felt fulfilled by any of it. In that way, my purpose in life was gone. I had lost my mojo.

LOOKING FOR MY MOJO

There was one person I could always count on to boost my energy and give me a fresh perspective—and that was Tony Robbins. It had been seven years since I'd last been to one of his seminars. Fortunately, an upcoming event in January 2015 was Tony's Business Mastery seminar, a five-day program I'd never been to. Now was definitely the time! I was hoping for a breakthrough that would give me clarity and reenergize my vision for the next decade.

As I sat in anticipation among hundreds of attendees, my mind began to wander. My thoughts entered a continuous loop:

Can I get my hunger back for i9?
Do I even want to do this anymore?
If I don't, what should I do next?"

I had been driven by my desire to make i9 a game-changer in the amateur sports industry. And we had done it.

So, what was the problem?

At that moment, Tony paused, and with his commanding voice, he uttered these words: "Success without fulfillment is ultimate failure." Oh my God, I felt as though he had just spoken directly to me. The guy who was my mentor—my greatest inspiration in life—had just called me a failure. Nobody else around me seemed negatively impacted by his words, but I sat there devastated for the next thirty minutes. What he said hit me right between the eyes. And he was totally right. Then came his knockout punch.

"If you no longer have passion for what you're doing, you should just get out and sell the company. You owe it to yourself, and you owe it to your company!"

What? Did he just tell me to quit? It shocked me, because I'd never heard Tony use the word "quit" about anything. But here he was, opening the door for me to break loose and sell my company. I could stop being stuck in a company I'd outgrown! It made total sense to me, and I was relieved to hear it. I loved i9 Sports with all my heart, and I would never have done anything to hurt it. But I was, in essence, hurting it by fulfilling my own selfish needs by remaining with it.

THE BEST EXIT STRATEGY

On the third day of the seminar, a bolt of lightning hit me when Tony shared the concept of selling a company to its *employees*, a so-called ESOP (Employee Stock Ownership Plan).

As he explained it, an ESOP provides significant tax benefits while allowing you to receive desired liquidity without selling to a competitor or third party. You could gradually transition the ownership of the company over a period of time and remain as actively involved in the business as you wanted to be. Meanwhile, you could avoid giving out confidential information to a competitor or other potential buyers.

In other words, an ESOP allows you to cash out, take your chips off the table, defer taxes on that money, and still stay in control of the company—while making your employees happy with a windfall of cash—making it profitable for everyone. As Tony finished, he said he had sold his San Diego-based company, Robbins Research, exactly this way three months earlier. This, I thought, was the Holy Grail! And with Tony suggesting it, he was giving me permission *and* the resources to take the next step. I felt as though I received the blessing from the man I admired the most.

If I took that route, I wouldn't have to feel guilty about selling i9, because I would be leaving it in good hands—with the employees I trusted. I would be free—no longer subject to the pressures and obligations, but still able to profit from my many years of dedication. And I would preserve my legacy.

Tony announced that he wanted to give the attendees access to the same investment bank that introduced him to the ESOP concept and helped architect his transaction, a boutique firm named CSG Partners LLC. It specialized in mergers and acquisitions, and they had a hospitality table right outside the door. I can tell you that during the break, I ran out of the auditorium to the CSG table, where I met the firm's managing director, Richard Harmon, and the co-founder, Alex Meshechok. It seemed as if I met all the ESOP criteria. I was bouncing off the walls with excitement.

Later that night I called Nadine, talking a hundred miles a minute about the ESOP. The enthusiasm in my voice, and all the details I gave her about cashing out and deferring income taxes, made her want to hear more. "Tony did an ESOP himself! It's legit!" I shouted.

Nadine liked the idea and wanted to hear more about it, though she was as cautious as she was enthusiastic.

Brian was totally on board with it because he liked the idea of rewarding our employees—putting their skin in the game, so to speak. I invited him to attend Tony's next event, which was scheduled for London. He said:

> From a business perspective, Business Mastery pulled me up out of the weeds to a 30,000-foot view of our business and helped me identify a list of the ten key actions we needed to take as a company in the six to twelve months ahead. Since Frank had previously attended, it also gave us a common language and tool set to implement the changes.

> Frank and I didn't sit together so we could get maximum benefit from the group breakout sessions with other attendees. However, over beef pot pie in the little pub down the street, we had a blast comparing notes and discussing what an ESOP might look like. It was full steam ahead.

THE DAMAGE DONE

Two months later, following up on the exuberance I felt from Business Mastery, I attended Tony's Unleash the Power Within program. It would be an unlikely place for me to find clarity about what I was doing to my body with those diet pills. At one point on the first afternoon of the seminar, Tony talked about how 19 million people drug themselves with antidepressants, though the effectiveness of the drugs is highly questionable. "Biochemistry," Tony said, "can be instantly changed *without* drugs, which may sound like hyperbole." He went on to discuss how he has proven over the decades that a drastic change in physiology through exercise or breathing can totally alter our mindsets almost instantaneously.

But we take on these identities of diseases and feel we're doomed. Are there people for whom only medication can make a difference? Yes, but I'd say it's rare, a small percentage. And 75 percent of people who take antidepressants are still depressed.

There I sat, weighing 163 pounds, the lowest I'd been since college, with a diet pill stashed in the front pocket of my jeans! The guilt of it washed over me in waves. I knew I was addicted. I knew I had been lying to myself. There was no question that phendimetrazine had played a major role in my severe burnout. I had been driven to take it in a desperate desire to lose weight. I knew my health was steadily deteriorating. And I had no one to blame but myself.

But everything changed that night during the seminar's climactic firewalk—a metaphor, as I mentioned earlier, for breaking through the thing you fear most. During the twelve hours leading up to the walk, I finally hit what Tony called the threshold of pain—the point at which you can't go on any longer living the same way. Change is no longer a should. It's a must. I realized I was more than just some number on a scale. My weight did not define me! And I didn't need a drug to make myself feel better.

As I finished the firewalk that night, I threw that last pill into the fire and vowed never to take the drug again. I never did, but the damage was already done. I was a ticking time bomb.

THE TOP OF THE MOUNTAIN

- There are always two businesses you've got to manage—the one you're in and the one you're becoming. Don't forget to work on both!
- Speed kills. Don't continue expanding your business while there are cracks in the foundation. Get your infrastructure fixed first!
- If you are a start-up kind of guy, delegate the administrative side to someone else.
- When your vision for your business is complete, it's time to create a new one or consider moving on.
- The measure of wealth you achieve is in proportion to the impact you make on others' lives—the value you provide to someone else.
- "Success without fulfillment is the ultimate failure."
- "If you no longer have passion for what you're doing, you should just get out and sell the company. You owe it to yourself, and you owe it to your company."

Chapter Thirteen

THE CHOICE TO SELL

In April 2015, the cumulative effect of Tony's seminars and my deep lack of fulfillment converged. I woke up on the morning of April 23rd with incredible clarity. The first thought that came to me was *Today is the day. It's time to sell i9 Sports!* That idea was incredibly freeing, as I'd never made a decision with such conviction immediately upon waking up. This was not an emotional impulse. It felt like a guided decision. I'd thought it through long enough. It was absolutely the right decision for both the business and for me.

A month later, at the suggestion of my private life coach, Sara, I penned a love letter to i9. The letter was an exercise designed to help me get closure on my decision to sell my company and a way for me to tell my dream business exactly how I felt about it.

I began to write, starting with the sale of ABA and the dream of going national:

Dear i9,

We pumped $500,000 into "birthing" a company that began with a challenging staff and an over-broad brand ambition—to serve both adult and youth sports.

And even though you were bleeding terribly the first three years, losing hundreds of thousands, I refused to give up on you. I knew you would pull through. Many would've quit on you then, but I had zero doubts about your survival.

We were desperate, but not hopeless. You pulled through, thanks to the consulting efforts of Joe Mathews and Brian Sanders, the momentum of a thriving economy in 2006 to 2007, and the decisions I made for you in improving your staff.

And on I went, retelling the story of i9's history in a soliloquy of gratitude:

Maybe it was fate, luck, or a combination of both, but you gained enough momentum (monthly recurring income) to survive the Great Recession. The secret to our success was the congruent need for growth. Never sitting still, we fed off of each other's desire to grow, try out new things, and persevere in the face of danger.

We prevailed in every challenge, our success the result of a team effort. I could never have done it without the total support of Nadine and an office team led by Kim—or without the drive to grow beyond my comfort zone. (In that department, I'd have to credit Tony Robbins for sure!)

My vision for you was to change an industry—to raise standards. Of course, that would inevitably inspire copycat leagues nationwide.

All in all, I put my heart and soul into your success. In fact, I sometimes put you first, ahead of nearly everything in the early years, and I sacrificed spending time with Nadine and the kids.

And now, rewarded with a lifestyle far grander than any I could ever have envisioned (traveling a long way from that run-down, roach-infested apartment of my childhood), I was ready to turn the page and begin a new chapter.

Yes, I was selling my baby. I finished the letter this way:

The brand is bigger than any one person. And you've grown as big and gone as far as I'm supposed to take you. If I continued, it would be without inspiration, and only for the money.

And that's not why I started you. You want more than that. While nobody will ever love you as much or know you as well as I do, it's time for us to go our separate ways, because I can't provide what you need for the next stage of your life.

With much love and gratitude,

—Me.

IGNORING THE PULL ON MY HEARTSTRINGS

With my end goal of selling i9 set in stone, I wrestled with the choice about the best way to do it. I was torn in half. I knew it was the right decision, but parting with the company nonetheless pulled on my heartstrings. The choice came down to two scenarios.

Should I sell i9 to a private equity firm, pay all the taxes, and cash out *immediately*? That would jeopardize the jobs of my employees, all of whom were people I adored and who had helped me rise to the top. Or should I sell i9 via an ESOP, with all the tax-saving benefits, which would also allow me to keep the staff intact, making them wealthy in the long run? The risk to me would be getting paid out little by little, if at all, rather than in one lump sum. I'd also have to remain indefinitely attached to a company that I had grown apart from.

It came down to doing the right thing for my employees versus doing the most expedient and profitable thing for me. I wanted to weigh the options a little longer, so I put the decision on hold, knowing I wouldn't have to take any action until September, which would still allow me to sell i9 by year's end.

INTERLUDE AND OVERLOAD

In the meantime, that summer, Nadine and I decided to take the kids on a trip to France and England, a special getaway to celebrate our twentieth wedding anniversary. When we got to Paris, I began to feel rather sick, a little feverish. Within a few hours, my temperature had rocketed to 103. I was burning up. But then, oddly, a few hours later, I suddenly started shivering, drenched in cold sweat, my temperature plummeting to 95 degrees.

Back and forth it went. I'd feel fine for a few hours, thinking I was on the mend, and then suddenly my temperature would go dramatically up and then back down again and again. I thought I was going to die. It was like Superman being touched by Kryptonite. I didn't know it at the time, but my adrenal glands were very weak due to the years of taking those diet pills. Despite how I felt, I continued to go out with our tour guides every day, all day, over the course of a full week.

By the fourth day, when our tour guides took us to Omaha Beach, I had pushed it too far. It was the moment of the trip I had looked most forward to, since my grandfather Walter had fought in World War II and had been wounded during the Battle of the Bulge. On the beach that day, I felt a mixture of pride and sadness for the loss of life. The next stop took us to the nearby Normandy American Cemetery, filled with acres of tombstones from World War II. It was an unseasonably hot day, and as the sun beat down on me, I could feel my temperature rising again.

During a ceremonial rendition of "Taps," I suddenly started seeing black spots, and I started to sway. My legs felt like jelly and I nearly passed out. I knew something was very wrong. By the time we got back to Paris, I was feeling really sick again, coughing and weak. A doctor was sent to my room and diagnosed me with pneumonia. It seems that my immune system had been massively compromised, a result of my long-term use of phendimetrazine, which had turned me into a disaster waiting to happen. I now had a horrendous wet, rattling cough, and sinus issues that the physician treated with loads of pills and liquid prescriptions.

> **"OUR WORST NIGHTMARE WAS BEING LEFT WITH THE THOUGHT: WHAT IF WE HAD NOT TAKEN THAT CHANCE?"**

Despite what was happening to me, I didn't want to prematurely end our sixteen-day trip, so I trudged on feeling lousy. It would take me months to fully recover from the pneumonia.

COMING TO GRIPS

By the end of summer 2015, as usual, I was running with my head down, consumed by one priority: How was I going to exit i9 Sports? I was still dealing with an immense amount of guilt surrounding the decision. I reflected on how my ABA years had been my happiest ones in the sports business—when it was just Kim and the guys in that small office on Oakfield Drive. We had grown by leaps and bounds and had so much fun doing it, able to implement changes quickly without committees, task forces, or franchise advisory councils.

But despite contemplating how I was going to sell, Nadine was entirely supportive of it.

> *I was definitely supportive of Frank selling the business, because it was something he had a strong conviction about. And throughout our lives, our attitude was that if we believe in something, then we go ahead and do it with no regret. Our worst nightmare was being left with the thought: What if we had not taken that chance?*
>
> *But selling the company was a decision that he struggled with more than I thought he would. He was very close to Brian and Kim and the entire team and cared about them. He didn't just want to sell the company to some random investor who would come in and clean house. That weighed on him more than anything.*

My CPA opposed the idea of selling via ESOP. "Look," he told me, "by not cashing out immediately, it's going to take the company years to pay you back (if they can ever pay you back in full at all). This will only tie you to i9 indefinitely, just for the benefit of saving on income taxes. You'll get no relief from stress, especially when the next franchisee crisis occurs."

He further argued that Nadine and I were not the type of people who wanted to fly around in private jets, nor did we need to support umpteen generations financially. His vote was to "sell the damn company to a private equity firm and get out, because life is too short!" Although it wasn't what I wanted to hear, I loved Bill's blunt feedback, which took all of the emotion out of decision-making. While I couldn't argue that he was 100 percent correct about my personal interests, what about the employees? Bill's detached viewpoint was that I had no obligation to my team. They were, he said, just as free to quit at any time as I was free to sell the company whenever I wished. That was true.

Fired up by his point of view, I reached out to dozens of private equity firms that had contacted me over the years. Multiple offers came in. The best offer I got was a very lucrative deal from a firm in the Northeast that also included a continuing stake of 10 percent in the company. While I wasn't quite sure yet what the company was worth, we were off to a good start, and it made my decision more difficult.

TO ESOP OR NOT

Ready to weigh the ESOP option, I called CSG Partners to schedule a face-to-face meeting at our office. The more I thought about it, the more ESOP-ing the company just felt like the right thing to do. To take the emotion out of it, I took out a sheet of paper and did a pros and cons comparison, just as I did when Nadine and I were contemplating moving to Florida nearly twenty years earlier. The decision became abundantly clear. Just a few weeks later, on September 2, 2015—my forty-seventh birthday—I signed the agreement with CSG to begin the ESOP process. The truth was that I had been leaning heavily toward doing the ESOP all along. However, the next several months were a living hell for Kim, Brian, and me as we compiled all the due-diligence data required for the ESOP. We didn't go a day without a conference call or multiple emails back and forth with CSG, lawyers, accountants, and trustees.

All this background prep was being conducted confidentially, without the knowledge of our other employees or franchisees. The secrecy was necessary to make sure the deal went through without outsiders knowing about it or employees getting caught up in the excitement.

The ESOP process progressed steadily—with its most important goal being to come up with a valuation of the company. After crunching all the data, CSG concluded that i9 was worth approximately 50 percent more than the offer sheet I had gotten from the private equity firm. Best of all, we could legally defer all the taxes. It was a slam-dunk decision.

CSG's goal was to pay me a small portion in cash up front by securing a loan that i9 would take out and then repay, along with the remaining balance. Nadine and I were elated.

AN UNFORGETTABLE NEW YEAR'S EVE

Two weeks later, I got the call I'd been waiting for from CSG. They had identified a company that was interested in loaning i9 the money to pay me for the ESOP. It was a firm based in the Washington, D.C., area that specialized in providing debt and equity capital to support buyouts, acquisitions, recapitalizations, and other ownership liquidity needs. Although the loaner company was actually a private equity firm, they understood that I wasn't selling i9 outright to them. Yet they were extremely interested and wanted to close by the end of the year.

On the night of December 8, 2015, I was driving in the car with my kids. Sitting at a traffic light, I noticed an email come in on my phone with the subject line: "THE OFFER." The lump in my throat was the size of an apple, and the moment was electric. That email was going to change all our lives.

I expected the cash upfront offer to fall within the range projected by CSG, but here was a lump-sum cash payment of more than triple what we expected—with the remaining amount, including stock options, paid out over several years by i9 Sports equivalent to the valuation. Wow.

I was speechless. While this was far from a done deal, the very first thought that came to my mind was *Tony bleeping Robbins!* He had done it again. He had offered a life-changing strategy. Unbelievable. Brian and Kim would benefit tremendously from the ESOP too, as I had given both of them generous amounts of i9 stock years earlier.

And then, on the afternoon on December 31st, the deal was done. I could hardly believe it: i9 was officially an ESOP, a company owned by its employees.

Quite a way to end the year!

WHEN YOU MAKE THE CHOICE TO SELL

- Be ready to deal with internal turmoil, guilt, and nostalgia about the start-up days.
- Prepare yourself to come to grips with what kind of stress you can handle with regard to your team.
- Work out the means to sell that will not only meet your own personal and financial goals, but will mirror your values as well.

Chapter Fourteen

TAKING STOCK

With the ESOP a done deal, I felt incredibly indebted to Tony Robbins. Were it not for him talking so passionately about the ESOP strategy at the Business Mastery presentation the previous January, I might never have known about it or profited from his knowledge. Through a mutual connection, I wrote Tony an email, thanking him for the profound impact he'd had on me over the years:

> *Just hours ago, I closed on my ESOP transaction as a result of what you said at Business Mastery back in January. Tony, the business that so few people believed in got valued way beyond my wildest dreams, a life changing deal for me, my family, and employees!*

And Tony wrote right back, congratulating me and telling me he was touched by the note. Three months later, at a Robbins event, I finally got to go backstage and meet the man who had had such a huge impact on my life. There he was—all six feet, seven inches of him! My daughter and I walked toward him to give him a big hug and a handshake, getting lost in his huge frame.

When I started to remind him about my ESOP sale, his eyes lit up, and with a giant smile, he replied, "Can you believe how amazing an ESOP is? I am so happy for you—I know the amount was outstanding!" I was stunned when he also remembered the exact number!

SUCCESS MAKERS

Back at home after the seminar, I began to think more and more about the multitude of factors that had contributed to the success of i9. In my decades of experience, this fact was certain: One of the secrets to success is a commitment to personal development. Whether it's reading and applying knowledge from dozens of self-help books, listening to Tony Robbins CDs, going to his events, or attending industry conferences, the greatest investment you'll ever make is an investment in yourself!

Why? Because self-awareness is the key to growth.

- You learn to identify what drives you forward, to envision a better future, and identify exactly how to fulfill your dreams.

- Along the way, you also learn to establish key connections and partnerships that will further your success.

- You gain perspective on your strengths and weaknesses. You accept feedback and coaching.

- You cancel out the fear that stops you from taking risks.

Tony always says, "Proximity is power," and I believe that being in his seminar community strengthened and focused me, allowing me to step up my game to match others who were determined to fulfill their full potential too. I realized that my future growth depended upon being around people who were just as passionate about their own growth and self-discovery as I was.

THE DEAL IS DONE!

One early afternoon in February 2016, while I was keeping myself busy sorting out boxes in the garage of our new home—we had sold the giant Miller Road house—my lawyer Stan called me with *the* news. The company loaning the money to fund the ESOP was sending over the approval documents, and a wire transfer would hit my account shortly thereafter.

For the next hour, I sat alone in the garage while Nadine and the kids were still unpacking and workers buzzed around putting finishing touches on the house. I couldn't stop thinking about my journey, from beginning with ABA up through the present with i9 Sports. I thought about all the struggles, all the times I wanted to quit so badly, and the near-fatalities of the business. But I had persevered and was about to be rewarded for running with my head down, as I had done so long ago.

When my cell phone rang again, I shot up. "The deal is done, Frank!" exclaimed Stan. "Go check your bank account online!" Nervously, I hung up and logged on from my phone in the garage. And there it was. Sitting tucked away in the garage, alone, I quietly broke down in tears, overwhelmed with gratitude.

Seeing the actual funds sitting in an account sure did feel nice, but my emotional reaction was prompted by a flood of overwhelming thankfulness for all that i9 Sports had meant to me. I went back in the house and shared the happy news with Nadine. It

"WITHOUT THEIR HARD WORK AND SUPPORT, I COULDN'T HAVE DONE IT."

was a joyous moment for both of us, as we reminisced about all we'd been through to get that far. My goal had always been about fulfilling my mission in life, my purpose, creating i9, and making a real difference in people's lives. And we had done it.

Sharing the great news with my staff was the best part. The nervous energy was high in the building as I stood in front of them with my family looking on. I couldn't help but feel incredibly grateful to all of them. Without their hard work and support, I couldn't have done it. As I began to speak about how far we'd come, the intense concern on their faces grew more pronounced. Was I about to tell them that I'd sold the company?

As a matter of fact, that's exactly what I did. "Yes, I've sold the company, but I've sold it to YOU!" At that point, we unveiled a banner announcing that i9 Sports Corporation was now an employee-owned company. And then, through the applause and smiles, I could tell that everyone was relieved, though they had no idea how dramatically the ESOP would impact them financially. Everyone left on a high that day, and Nadine, the kids, and I went home to digest all the incredible news.

FACING REALITIES

Despite all the great news, a very uneasy feeling churned inside of me as the months went by. I began to feel weighed down by the financial obligation to our equity lender. Yes, they had advanced me part of the sale price of i9. But if the company didn't hit certain quarterly benchmarks and financial ratios to comply with the contract, I could, in fact, lose the company—including the balance of what i9 owed me. Not to mention that my stock options would be worth nothing.

It wasn't as though the financial benchmarks were going to be that difficult to meet in the near term; however, my focus had always been on innovation, and now all my attention turned to i9 being in compliance with our funding equity partner. I became strictly about the numbers—the opposite of what had been my winning formula in business for over two decades. As time passed, I began attending our monthly finance meetings with my attention focused solely on i9 complying with the financial benchmarks.

The positive, motivating leader I'd been was now in it for the money. That's not who I was or ever had been, and I was becoming depressed. Considering my overall good fortune, I also felt embarrassed. Who could I possibly talk to who would understand or sympathize with me? *Nobody*, I thought. What could they say? "Oh, poor Frank. He's wealthy and depressed." Yeah, we did have a bunch of zeros in our account. It was money that we invested wisely with financial planners. But it seemed that I was tethered to the company more now than ever, and my feeling of being alone at the top had reached an entirely new level.

My internal turbulence connected to ESOP-ing i9 left me exhausted. By spring 2016, I was severely depressed and chronically fatigued. Even though I had chosen to sell i9, I still felt a deep sense of loss. I had set my company free—and it no longer needed me. What was I going to do now? What was my purpose? And what was I going to do about how bad I felt physically? It had been a year since I had stopped taking diet pills, and my weight had ballooned back up to nearly two hundred pounds. I wasn't sleeping at night, and the insomnia added to my general feeling of weakness.

I was low on energy, mentally unfocused, and having short-term memory problems. I had to choose my words carefully before speaking, because I had trouble coming up with even common, simple words. I had hit rock bottom. It was time to seek medical help.

The functional medicine physician I saw in South Tampa explained that, after all those years of diet pills, I had adrenal fatigue syndrome. My adrenal glands were exhausted and unable to produce adequate quantities of hormones such as adrenaline and cortisol. The condition was affecting my memory, my ability to sleep, and my desire to work. In layman's terms, my glands had "flatlined" due to the amphetamines, which explained the burnout I had first experienced back in 2011.

As a result, I now had a weakened immune system and was much more susceptible to infections and colds. That explained coming down with pneumonia a year earlier and also why I was so lethargic and depressed and had so much trouble focusing. As I learned, they call it brain fog—difficulty coming up with simple words in my head. I was a mess. I would need months of routine exercise, supplements, vitamins, and tons of rest to reverse the damage caused by phendimetrazine—and it would be nearly one year before my adrenal glands and immune system fully returned to normal.

Nadine had noticed that when I was taking diet pills, my personality was altered—I was seemingly stuck in my own head and abrupt at times. She would tell me the effect the medicine was having on me, but I didn't want to hear any of it. The weight management doctor had continued to prescribed it on and off for nearly nine years, in spite of the dangers.

Unfortunately, we sometimes only see what's on the outside, with no idea about what's really going on. The ridiculousness of it all is that when I was on phendimetrazine, downing pre-workout caffeine drinks, and working out like a madman, I looked physically fit, but I was a mess inside. Yet nobody could see that—not even me! It was all "Wow, look how amazing you look!" It was one great big lie. I had become obsessed with my business image, and I paid a steep price for it. I allowed that pill to rule me and even jeopardize my life. I've learned a lot from looking back at the past, understanding how it all happened—though until recently I wasn't willing to talk about it. The fact that I'm able to talk about it now is—for me—a sign of growth and self-renewal.

And if there's any lesson in this, it's that there truly is no magic pill to solve our problems. Worse yet, as with any drug you shouldn't use, you either pay now or pay later. And when it's later, you pay a much bigger price.

TAKING STOCK

- The greatest investment you'll ever make is an investment in your own personal development.
- Self-awareness is the key to growth: Identify what drives you forward and establish key connections on the way.
- Surround yourself with people that will challenge you to reach your full potential.
- Financial achievement does not protect you from feeling lonely at the top.
- A willingness to talk openly about your weakness is a sign of growth and self-renewal.
- There is no magic pill to solve your problems, and you don't need to suffer alone. Seek professional help when you need it.

Chapter Fifteen

TO LOVE AND INSPIRE

Nine months after turning i9 Sports into an ESOP, I continued to struggle between successfully completing my mission as the founder and quitting the business completely. Throughout my life, I had never allowed quitting to be an option for me. For decades, I had identified i9 as my purpose in life. And you can't walk away from your purpose, right? But as my CPA Bill had predicted a year earlier, the ESOP had become a noose around my neck that would tighten anytime there was a crisis at the office.

And in fact, with our management team dealing with revolving doors concerning both franchise salespeople and customer service center reps, there seemed to be a carousel of problems that kept spinning—which irritated me now more than ever. Even though both of the personnel issues would be resolved over time through outsourcing, my reaction to all the chaos was negative, made all the more painful because I was a financially tied spectator.

I'm not saying that I could've done a better job. That was definitely not the case. But

"WHAT WAS THE PRICE OF HAPPINESS?"

having significant dollars tied to the business that no longer needed me only reinforced my conviction that this arrangement with i9 was not going to last. The question became—could I hang in there for another four or five years to get paid the balance the company owed me and then sell the ESOP to maximize my stock options? What was the price of happiness?

And since the sale of i9 seemed inevitable, I began to project ahead and contemplate—what's next for me? It was a question I hadn't asked myself since graduating college twenty-six years earlier. One idea: Because Tony Robbins had such a huge impact on my life, I felt the need to give back to him by becoming part of Tony's Senior Leadership Team.

So, during the last half of 2016, I signed up for everything Robbins-related to give myself the tools and resources I'd need. Through it all, my primary focus was to master the tools that would allow me to help others and share with them the winning formula that had made i9 such a success. One of Tony's programs hit home particularly hard. A new me returned home from the one called Date with Destiny. The wisdom I took away was extensive.

- If you're not living a life congruent with your values, you're going to be unhappy. The fulfillment of riches does not eliminate that unhappiness; it's only a temporary fix. (So, in my case, by staying tied to i9 Sports, I was paying a dear price.)

- Change your story; change your life: My story was that I grew up in a broken home, with little financial means and a damaged sense of self-confidence. All that caused me significant pain in almost every aspect of my life. But my realization was that life happens *for us*, not *to us*. If you're going to blame anyone for all the bad things that happened to you, you need to "blame" them for all the good things too—such as the inner strength that comes from pain. It's all a *gift* to be grateful for. Transform your old story with a flood of gratitude for everyone who has ever entered your life. I could see that every person and event had been part of my experience for a reason. I may not have understood it at the time (and may never know why), but there was a definite logic to it all.

- Create a compelling future: What you focus on, the words you use, and your physiology determine your emotional condition. You can change how you feel in seconds by changing your focus, language, and body state. In other words, the quality of your life is nothing but the quality of your emotions, which are in your control.

- Realize you are here to have fun, to love, to inspire, and to give to others.

- Your purpose never stands still. It's a living thing that is always evolving. I could see now that i9 Sports was nothing more than the *vehicle* I'd been using to do inspirational work for myself and others. The vehicle could change—though my purpose would remain the same.

In the end, I didn't actually know what my next mission in life would be. I just knew it wasn't i9 Sports anymore.

STEPPING AWAY

I was finally at peace with moving on. The very next week, I sat down with Brian.

"I'm so proud of what we've accomplished, but I think it's time for me to move on. You and the team," I continued, "are doing an incredible job for the company. I have total confidence in you. But I'm no longer needed and have felt out of place here for a while now. Therefore, I want to close the ESOP, sell the company to a private equity firm, and exit the organization."

He was definitely taken by surprise.

The plan was to ESOP, to give the employees a stake in the business. But Frank was going to stay on as chairman of the board, me as CEO, and we would continue in the same work pattern as always. Frank, as father of the brand, would provide counsel as I needed it, thereby causing no alarm to franchisees. But when he came to me that day, he said he'd been struggling with his role and the value he brought to the business, which no longer aligned with what he wanted to do.

It was true that the business didn't need me at the same level that it once did. And being true to myself, I knew it was time to go. I wanted to take a breather, reflect on where I'd been, and explore what my next step in life was going to be. As I went on, I further explained that I'd been feeling unfulfilled for a long time—and alluded to the fact that I had battled depression over it, without saying those words exactly.

Brian finally asked: "Is this really what you want?" And I told him it was.

As expected, Brian was a total professional, a true empathetic leader and friend, focusing on what was best for my health and well-being rather than how my leaving would potentially affect his career should I sell to an outsider.

Kim's reaction to the news? "I cried," she said. "I couldn't understand it. As the days and weeks passed, getting used to the idea of Frank leaving was like going through the stages of grief. It was shock, then anger."

But she accepted it, and like Brian, added how grateful she was for everything I'd ever done, and how life for her and her family far exceeded her own expectations. This made me feel so thankful for all her hard work, and ours, which had led to the company's success.

I left the office after that meeting with a giant gorilla off my back.

Now both Brian and Kim finally knew what I had kept to myself for too long. Within days, I held a conference call with the team at CSG Partners, who walked me through the process of closing the ESOP and selling the company.

Alex shared with me that under the current market conditions, now was as good a time as any. "The mergers and acquisition market is frothy now, and there is quite an appetite for franchise companies. Because i9 is such a solid company, I'm confident we can find you a good buyer."

"How long will it take?" I asked, expecting him to say upward of a year.

"Six months, give or take. Assuming we can get all the documentation from Kim and Brian again, like we did for the ESOP, we're looking at a closing by the end of summer." It was a timeline that far exceeded my expectations, one that would allow me to get paid the rest of what i9 owed me, along with any value for my stock options. In addition, the eligible employees would receive an unexpected windfall. Two big questions hung in the balance. Who was going to buy us, and how much were they willing to pay?

Because we had such a solid working relationship with the guys who financed the original loan to i9, it made sense to reach out to them first to see if they had any interest, which they immediately did. While a few other private equity firms remained interested, it seemed nobody was going to outbid our original lender, as the counteroffers continued to rise. Negotiations went back and forth between CSG and our equity lender over several weeks until I got *the* call from Alex on May 26, 2017.

"Frank, I've got some news for you. We just got the *best and final offer*. We're not going to get another penny out of them. We have pushed them to the limit. What do you want to do?"

"DONE! Close the deal, Alex!" I yelled back into the phone. Alex agreed that it was an excellent offer and I'd be crazy not to accept it.

The final condition of the sale was that I'd agree to reinvest a portion of my proceeds back into i9 Sports to show good faith and belief in i9's future. This meant I'd still technically be an owner of the company until the investment firm decided to sell it. Even better, most of my proceeds were exempt from taxes since we did the ESOP first, though I would be generously sharing millions with the employees. All in all, for everyone, it would be financially life-changing!

Who could have ever predicted that the business on life support in 2005 would bring us the success it did? Tony Robbins had often said, "We overestimate what we can do in a year and underestimate what we can accomplish in a decade." That rang so true in this case.

The next day, Kim called to remind me of a conversation we'd had roughly fourteen years earlier. She said, "I don't know if you're going to remember this, but there was a day back during the ABA years when it was just me, you, and the guys in the office. The Florida Lottery was some crazy number, and we all talked about what we would do if we won. But you surprised us all when you said, 'I'd never want to win the lottery because if I did, I'd be cheating myself out of making it on my own.' Do you remember that?"

"I sure do, Kim. It was true. I didn't want it to steal the joy of doing it on my own or be remembered for just being lucky."

"Well, last night when I got home, right after you told me that the company was sold, I turned to my husband, and said, 'Frank never wanted to hit the lottery, so he could do it on his own, and sure enough, he did it! Unbelievable.'"

THE END OF AN ERA

In the summer of 2017, while on the verge of finalizing the sale, I was scheduled to speak at our national meeting being held at the Hilton Hotel across from Disney Springs in Orlando. We now had more than 140 franchisees operating nine hundred locations across thirty states, making i9 Sports the dominant brand name in the industry.

As I walked into the convention hall, with nearly two hundred people waiting to hear me, memories from past national meetings ran through my head, along with a flash of thoughts about the tough times—starting the business, the struggles we had, the fabulous triumphs, and everything in between.

The energy from the franchisees and i9 employees was incredibly positive. I looked out over a sea of smiling faces and head nods as I delivered my twenty-minute speech. It was a combination of company history and inspiration, and it focused on how we could move into the future, stronger than ever, with unlimited potential. When I finished the speech on a high note, it felt incredible to draw a roar from the crowd.

All in all, the triumph of the morning was especially meaningful because it felt like total redemption from the response I'd gotten at the national meeting four years earlier in San Antonio. Throughout the rest of the meeting, one franchisee after another came up to me, gave me a hug, and shared how i9 had changed their lives for the better. Some shed tears or got choked up. Everyone was so appreciative.

After twenty-two years in the sports business, fifteen of them with i9 Sports, I felt only admiration for my entire organization of franchisees and employees, and I felt gratitude toward the company that had given me so much. As if emotions weren't running high enough, behind-the-scenes negotiations for the sale of i9 were now nearly finalized. I was ready to become a minority shareholder of the company, contribute as a board member, and support Brian, Kim, and the staff in any way I could.

My purpose at i9 Sports was complete. It would always be my baby, but it had grown up, gotten married, and now had kids of its own. I could thereafter be the loving, supportive grandparent—and admire it with much pride. I was touched by Brian's view of things:

When Frank created his company, he disrupted what had become a stale, inward-focused industry, town leagues that had been around for generations were driven by parental politics, local coaches, and league commissioners who were more interested in what they wanted than what was best for kids. It was all rinse and repeat, season after season. But Frank reclaimed youth sports and put a brand-new spin on it. He focused on creating a fun, convenient sports experience just for kids, and made it convenient for parents too. That's his legacy.

I was excited about stepping into the limited role as board member, giving strategic advice and providing guidance without the complications associated with running the company. All of it gave me a renewed energy I hadn't felt in years. There was only one thing left to do—*inform my employees with the news about the financial windfall they were about to receive!*

The morning I told them was one of the most gratifying moments in my entire professional life. As Nadine and I entered the training room, the eyes of all sixteen employees were wide as saucers.

I cut right to the chase. "Good morning everyone. I have some big news! i9 Sports has been acquired by an investment firm—a move that will grow the company and provide additional resources. Essentially, we are flip-flopping roles. When i9 first became an ESOP, I was the majority shareholder, and our investor was the minority. Now it will be the reverse."

At first, everyone looked stunned. Some went from happy and laughing to worried or blank expressions, while others were smiling through the fear. But the mood began to change as I shared with them that the sale of the company resulted in our stock price doubling and triggered a substantial distribution of additional shares to *them*!

In total, several millions of dollars would be distributed among the sixteen full-time (eligible) employees. The announcement of the cash giveaway was like putting the finishing touches on an absolute masterpiece of a company success that couldn't have been better scripted in Hollywood! It was nearly overwhelming.

Nadine was just as excited. "That day," she recalls, "was almost too good to be true. I cried the whole time. I was so touched that I almost couldn't get a grip. Frank had started with an idea for a local adult men's softball league, and it had changed and grown into a national youth sports franchise business. And years later, the team that had helped him build everything were all getting substantial bonuses. It was a Cinderella kind of story."

The franchisees viewed the acquisition of i9 as a victory, since outside ownership could provide the ready capital needed to expand the company's services and fuel its continued growth. This would, in turn, expand our services and ability to grow. As I drove home with Nadine from the office that afternoon, my son, Frankie, jokingly reminded me that for the first time in years, I was unemployed. And it felt so damn good!

TO LOVE AND INSPIRE

- If you are not living a life congruent with your values, you're going to be unhappy.
- Looking at your story with gratitude will change your story—and your life.
- The quality of your life is the quality of your emotions—which are under your control.
- You are here to have fun, to love, to inspire, and to give to others.
- Your purpose never stands still. It's always evolving.

Chapter Sixteen

THE WAR IS OVER

A week after the sale of i9, I had no regrets. I felt free. It was absolutely the right time for me. There was no sadness or remorse about it. Like any entrepreneur who leaves his business, I felt a range of emotions, from total gratitude and relief to uncertainty about the unknown. What would come next? What would it be like to no longer go into the office?

And despite having the ability to live off the interest from the sale of i9, I felt I was much too young to do that. I still wanted to work and be productive. While the changeover from full-time work was instantly satisfying, I admit that it also felt a little weird. Suddenly, there was no structure or obligation.

Meanwhile, Nadine and Taylor-Marie had gone on a getaway to a mystical place called the Miraval Arizona Resort & Spa, a wellness retreat tucked away in Tucson where you learn to become mindful of the present moment, disconnect from the stressors of daily life, and reconnect with nature. Hearing that it was such a spiritual place, I thought I would give it a try. As a bonus, my daughter would come along with me!

When we arrived and walked through the grounds, I felt the peace of the place. It was as if everything around us was moving in slow motion, as though time stood still. One of my private sessions involved a technique called Holographic Memory Resolution (HMR). It's an emotional reframing approach to therapy that allows you to access memories of past traumatic experiences or stressful events, while emphasizing the mind-body connection. I dug deep and connected with a dozen or so physical pains—some related to my health, others a result of stress—but all of them tied to events in my life that had left behind emotional bruises. Thanks to that session, I healed a number of emotion-related physical symptoms that reflected deep pain from the past, most notably a chronic neck pain that had been with me for decades (and I continue to be pain-free nearly three years later).

At some point during the eighty-minute session, the following words came to me loud and clear: *The war is over.* What a relief it was! At that very moment it dawned on me that I had been engaged in an epic struggle with myself for forty years. I had battled self-rejection, shame, guilt, and the fear of not being good enough. I was virtually disarming myself. I envisioned laying down a rifle and could even hear the sound of the metal from the weapon clank on the ground. It was absolutely the most freeing, liberating feeling I'd ever experienced.

I was no longer going to carry any of my parents' judgments or past baggage, which I had been unconsciously doing for years. I was never again going to need to comfort myself due to scarcity, nor punish myself for any shame or rejection I felt in the past. I resolved from that point forward I would only surround myself with people who could be supportive and loving, and who would enhance my happiness.

These people would inspire and motivate me. Likewise, *I* could also inspire and help others—to overcome rejection and doubt or any self-negating habit of the heart.

"WORRYING IS PRAYING FOR THINGS YOU DON'T WANT."

I learned that worrying is praying for things you don't want (a fear-based activity that focuses on the negative). And if you ignore your emotions, your emotions will ignore you. Squelching feelings that are meant to be felt and expressed, rather than suppressed, is a bad habit that often leads to depression.

As one of my instructors, a master practitioner of energy healing, advised, "Allow yourself to follow your purpose, even if it means that you struggle and make plenty of mistakes. When you love something, you need to keep doing it. Persevere! Don't stop a dream because you don't think you're good enough to attain it." This spiritual adventure was about healing, and I related it back to what "running with my head down" was all about. By turning inward and focusing, I would be able to reconnect with joy and hopefully pass it on to others.

I left Miraval disarmed, my defenses down. As I said, the war I never even realized I was fighting was finally over. And I celebrated the victory by beginning to do something I never imagined I could ever do—learn how to play the electric guitar! I could see that my job was to be happy with *myself* rather than only being focused on making others happy. While we are all put on earth to serve, we also need to pay attention to what brings us personal joy. Never again would I say I wasn't talented enough or too old to start. In less than two months of lessons (and some rigorous daily practice on my own), I had learned enough to play some riffs from the Beatles, Rolling Stones, Green Day, Def Leppard, Nirvana, and several others. Can you believe it? I was stretching myself in ways I'd never expected.

Soon after returning from Miraval, my son and I took a retreat of our own—to Yankee Stadium! I'll never forget it. As Frankie and I sat in the front row in section 104 of right field, within shouting distance of the Yankees' all-star rookie Aaron Judge, my mind reeled back to the past as I looked up at the upper-deck seats on the first-base side. I remembered my first trip to the original Yankee Stadium, sitting there in awe as an eleven-year-old with my mom and sister on my birthday. It was magical—just as it had been thirty-eight years ago. Only now I was sitting there with my *own* son!

I began to think about how truly fortunate I was. Despite all the twists and turns of life, I had wound up in such a lucky spot. As a kid, I never in a million years imagined that I would be blessed in this way—with a prosperous life and a loving family, with Nadine, and Taylor-Marie, and Frankie. After all, back in 1979, when I first visited the stadium, my home and school life seemed like one big losing battle.

However, though I couldn't see it at the time, the "game" wasn't over. Just like the Yankees, I battled back. I worked hard and expected more from myself than anyone else did. I threw everything I had into sports to create my own league, my own brand, and here I was so many years later, sitting with my sixteen-year-old son, appreciating my amazing journey.

That night, we witnessed the thrill of victory, an incredible Yankee comeback in the bottom of the eighth inning, which led to the Bronx Bombers winning the game. It was a perfect night of baseball, and much more than just a game to me. In some ways, it represented life. You practice and prepare, and then you go out there and compete. Sometimes you hit a home run; other times you strike out. There will be triumphant moments, but there will be heartbreaking ones too. And quite often, the difference between success and failure is nothing more than who can and can't persevere.

It's easy to blame the past or quit when things aren't going well. That's why so many people give up on their dreams. Tony Robbins believes that while problems are inevitable in life, we make the choice whether to suffer from them or not. I agree that how you react in the face of adversity ("coming in clutch" as they say in baseball) is what separates the winners from the losers in life. I can tell you that the time spent with my boy—the sights, sounds, and smells of the stadium, and the electric energy of a Yankee victory—was unforgettable. It simply doesn't get better than that. And it reminded me yet again of how lucky I am.

I HAD ARRIVED. BUT WHERE TO EXACTLY?

For the previous twenty-two years, my driving purpose in life had been running ABA and i9 Sports. They had been the total focus of my time and energy. The result had exceeded even my own expectations and had impacted millions of lives. I had now *arrived*, but where to exactly? I'd spent my entire adult life laser-focused on achieving business goals. I thought about how reaching the destination may not always be the best part of the journey.

And now, as my forty-ninth birthday approached, I felt it was time to do some soul-searching, to turn inward and learn more about myself. After five decades on the planet, it was time to lift myself away from the day-to-day routine of life and look beyond it.

WHEN THE WAR IS OVER AND YOU'RE READY TO LOOK BEYOND

- Surround yourself only with people who are supportive and enhance your happiness.
- Help and inspire others.
- Remember, worrying is praying for things you don't want.
- Don't suppress your feelings. If you ignore your emotions, your emotions will ignore you.
- Don't stop a dream because you don't think you're good enough to attain it.
- Often the difference between success and failure is nothing more than who *can* and *can't* persevere.
- "Problems are inevitable, but suffering is a choice."
- While we were all put on earth to serve, pay attention to what brings you personal joy.

Epilogue

RUNNING WITH MY HEAD UP

All my life I've been driven by the search for *purpose*—a quest that consumed me from the first time I asked my dad about it. He always told me that I'd find it—but in retrospect, it was never about *me* finding *it*. Your purpose in life is not like buried treasure. It's not something that you can actively search for. And it's not going to jump out at you.

Your purpose in life is a process of self-discovery, as you reflect on what makes you feel truly fulfilled. You discover your life's purpose when you recognize what gives you a sensational feeling of growth and contribution, what fulfills the needs of your soul.

Here's a clue how to get there: When you identify something you absolutely love to do and lose track of time while you're doing it, your purpose is showing up! You just need to pay attention to it. Expect that your purpose will likely be a *series* of pursuits that evolve as you move through your life. One pursuit leads to the next. And not every one of them will hit the bull's eye.

I often chose a pathway that didn't feel very good at the time I was on it. But I can see now that all the things I did were necessary steps that ultimately led to fulfilling my evolving purpose. In my case, everything started with my devout love of baseball. It was my life. Then, as a teenager, I took the job at Green Point Savings Bank. That job wasn't my ultimate purpose in life, but it provided a solid foundation in corporate culture, which was invaluable to me later as I created my own company—and just as significant, the guys at Green Point introduced me to the game of softball! My instant love of that game ignited a spark that eventually led to my own softball team.

Let's not forget the decade-long career in medical sales—one that I hated and felt trapped in for all those years. It taught me how to approach people, how to sell, and how to work autonomously. In fact, without the extreme dissatisfaction I felt toward medical sales, I might never have struck out on my own to create my own business, the ABA Softball League.

Then came all the challenges of creating my own start-up—the years working in the spare-bedroom home office, the endless hours on the phone, the printing and mailing in the wee hours, and the dozens of flights from Florida to Long Island to acquire more fields. I got rejected more often than not, but never giving up ultimately led to success. It may have seemed like a coincidence at the time that I stumbled upon the NFL's launch of a nationwide flag football league that took me in the direction of youth sports. But is there really any such thing as a total coincidence?

And it was those early days in Florida that eventually led to franchising an empire that has generated over $300 million, with the revenues benefiting hundreds of franchisees and thousands of employees. We changed the lives of our staff by creating i9 Sports and then selling it. But most important, we changed the lives of over two million kids, giving them an experience beyond the game and an opportunity to learn how to succeed in life through sports.

The one constant in all this was a simple philosophy—to live life with no regrets—which would ignite a spark for Nadine and me and lead to a life beyond our wildest dreams that has been filled with love and support through all the good times and bad, with our two kids at the center of our world. These are the pillars of happiness. And that, I know, is the very gift of life.

I hope that this book will inspire you to discover your own purpose in life—and pursue it relentlessly with absolutely no regrets.

ABOUT THE AUTHOR

Frank V. Fiume II is a pioneer in the youth sports industry and the founder of i9 Sports—the nation's first and leading franchisor of youth leagues and camps. Since 2003, i9 has generated over 300 million dollars—with more than two million participants in 900 communities across 30 states nationwide.

A baseball fanatic and native of Queens, New York, Frank graduated from St. John's University and began a career as a medical equipment sales rep, though he was determined to pursue his life's true purpose. So in 1995, he created his own adult men's softball league, ABA Sports. The start-up company quickly grew to over 900 teams in just six years, making it the largest adult sports organization on Long Island.

In 2003, Frank sold ABA in order to create i9 Sports, a business that catapulted him to national recognition and that *Entrepreneur* magazine ranked as the #1 children's fitness franchise. Frank has been featured on *Fox Business News*, *HBO Real Sports*, and in dozens of publications and national news media outlets, including *USA Today*, *Sports Illustrated*, and *The Wall Street Journal*.

Frank sold i9 Sports in 2017 to a private equity firm, but remains a minority shareholder and member of the board of directors.

He resides in the Tampa Bay area with his wife Nadine, their children Taylor-Marie and Frankie, and their Chocolate Lab Dillon.

@frankfiume

@frankfiumeii